We Know What You're Thinking

DARRELL BRICKER & JOHN WRIGHT
OF IPSOS REID

WE KNOW WHAT YOU'RE THINKING

From Dollars to Donuts:
Canada's Premier Pollsters
Reveal What Canadians
Think and Why

To Nina and Emily. You are always in my heart.
—D.B.

To Jennifer, my Super-hero; Josh, my Hockey-hero;
Olivia, my Soccer-hero; James, my Baseball-hero;
and Katie, my TV-journalist hero:
I love you for who you are and for whatever you aspire to be.
—J.W.

We Know What You're Thinking
© 2009 by Darrell Bricker and John Wright

All rights reserved.

Published by HarperCollins Publishers Ltd

First edition

No part of this book may be used or reproduced in any manner whatsoever without the prior written permission of the publisher, except in the case of brief quotations embodied in reviews.

HarperCollins books may be purchased for educational, business, or sales promotional use through our Special Markets Department.

HarperCollins Publishers Ltd
2 Bloor Street East, 20th Floor
Toronto, Ontario, Canada
M4W 1A8

www.harpercollins.ca

Library and Archives Canada Cataloguing in Publication

Bricker, Darrell Jay, 1961–
We know what you're thinking: from dollars to donuts—Canada's premier pollsters reveal what Canadians think and why/Darrell Bricker, John Wright.

ISBN 978-1-55468-261-4

1. Canadians—Attitudes.
2. Canada—Social conditions—21st century —Public opinion.
3. Canada—Civilization—21st century —Public opinion.
4. Public opinion—Canada.
I. Wright, John, 1957–
II. Title.
III. Title: We know what you're thinking.

HN110.Z9P8 2009   971.7   C2008-907940-X

DWF 9 8 7 6 5 4 3 2
Printed and bound in Canada

We Know What You're Thinking is printed on Ancient Forest Friendly paper, made with 100% post-consumer waste.

Book interior design by Sharon Kish

CONTENTS

Introduction / We Know

We'd like to say just trust us on that point. But then we actually know that only 40% of Canadians trust what we pollsters say (and that's not bad, given that CEOs are trusted by only 18%). Also, we don't know everything off the top of our heads—there are many things we do know, but not everything—so our publisher thought we should lay out some kind of credentials to back up the claim that we know what you're thinking.

You see, there are lots and lots of market research companies in Canada. Ipsos Reid is the biggest, though. We work on about $170 million worth of market research every year for the Canadian marketplace, and almost as much for the U.S. market. Our mothership corporation, Ipsos, is the second-largest market research company in the world, performing $1.6 billion (Canadian) worth of market and opinion research in over 100 countries. That's in just one year.

A lot of people ask us how we do our research. Some think that we throw questions out at an unsuspecting public and then try to sell their answers to clients. Well, okay, that occasionally happens—and we'd like to mention that we sell this research for a tenth of what it would cost our clients to discover it on their own. But that's seldom the way things normally go in the world of market research and opinion polls.

What *normally* happens is that somebody comes to us with a problem or a question. Most of the time, "somebody" is a corporation you have probably heard of, such as a big soft-drink company, a bank, a chocolate-bar maker, a drug manufacturer, a department store, a software developer . . . well, you get the idea. And they want to know how current and prospective customers view their products or services. They might want to know what people think of their reputation (even if they don't have much of one yet), or what customers think of a new ad campaign (before it's launched on television), or whether people consider the company's employees to be doing a good job (or whether employees themselves feel satisfied). Or the question might be something very specific, such as: Will food packaging attract more customers if it displays the words "free range" instead of "organic," or would it be more successful with both labels?

In short, we measure things. Not with a metre stick or a tape measure but by asking lots of questions in a survey format and then getting our computers to help "slice and dice" the results. The computer technology allows us to track the different responses we get from different audiences, age groups, income groups, or regions of the country. We then write up our findings, put together a nifty PowerPoint presentation, and ship it off to the client.

We've heard it alleged that all opinion pollsters do is produce results that tell the clients what they want to hear. Well, read our lips . . . oh, okay, you can't read our lips, but we'll ask the printer to make this bit as plain and clear as possible: *The truth matters.*

You see, market research is a very expensive tool. If you hired us and then manipulated us to tell your boss that a huge market existed for plaid wedding dresses when there actually wasn't one, it wouldn't take long for you and us, your research agency, to get the boot. So, truth matters. Sometimes clients expect a different result, and sometimes what we tell them disappoints them, but it's our job to give the results straight up. We may be mercenaries of a kind, but we're not missionaries, and we don't work to spread a particular gospel.

Some clients ask us to recruit so-called "real people," which means actual or plausible customers, patients, taxpayers, retirees, etc., who sit in a room and become that famous research tool, the "focus group." For a couple of hours, clients sit behind mirrored glass while in the room on the other side one of our research moderators asks people probing questions worked out in advance. The members of the focus group might say things that aren't quantifiable, that aren't representative of all people just like them, or that perhaps aren't even terrifically interesting, but it's useful for the clients to see and hear "real people" express unfiltered views. It's also a very useful way of teaching the researchers what needs to go into a full-length questionnaire aimed at gathering data.

Focus groups can sometimes be a challenge in themselves. Like the time a woman showed up at a 6:00 p.m. focus group meeting dressed in a clown suit and wearing full makeup because she was entertaining at an adult birthday party at 9:00. You can imagine what it was like for the moderator and the other nine members to sit in a room talking about the effects of cross-border trade with a clown interjecting that building another bridge between Canada and the United States would help ease the trade deficit between our two countries in real time.

And what about the clients? In that sealed-off room, they hear things that can send them into a tizzy. "What do you mean they don't understand what's inside the bottle? It's on the label!" . . ."I can't believe that their *one* bad customer service experience made them go somewhere else. I'll get the name of the person in our store and fire him tomorrow!" We've seen the disbelief when a client hears someone repeatedly referring to a chief competitor as having the best prices when the opposite is the case. Most of our clients see this as a learning experience and don't get too exercised over what people say; after all, it's vital to hear the unvarnished truth about what the public thinks. But then again, we have witnessed the paint company mixing engineer who, at the end of a focus group, went barging into the room just as people were getting ready to leave, ordered everyone back into their seats, and then went around the table with notebook in hand, correcting all of the misinformation he had heard about the product and the store chain. Needless to say, our client ensured that this employee was not involved in the rest of the focus group meetings that were convened in cities across Canada.

While the thousands of focus groups we conduct every year can be illuminating and even downright entertaining, it's our quantitative work that gets more attention—that is, the work of interviewing large groups of people and then tallying up their answers into survey results, which most people refer to as "polls." When you take into account how long we've have been involved in opinion research—Darrell 30 years and John 20, making a total of 50 years of looking at a bunch of data tables served up from interviewing people the night before, and then creating scads of other questions to use in interviews with more Canadians during the coming evening—you'll understand that we've seen the numbers on pretty much any and every subject imaginable: from vitamins to Viagra, taxes to tariffs.

On top of that, over the decades we've also held positions that include, between the two of us, working in government relations for a prime minister and a cabinet minister, working in advertising and media relations, lecturing at universities, and membership in many private, public, and not-for-profit boards of directors. So our work hasn't always been about questions or numbers, which is a good thing, because you've got to bring experience and perspective to the table when you try to help a client get from point A to point B.

We started working together at what was then a fairly modest polling company back in 1989. In those days, we had about $4.5 million in client billings and eleven senior staff. We learned from each other and traded stories about the exciting things we were doing. We knew every single company project, we partied hard like university students, and we pulled all-nighters for a week if we were doing something that was on the cutting edge. It was stimulating, it was exhilarating.

In the following years, Ipsos Reid became a household name because of the polling client relationships the company built with top media organizations in Canada and abroad. Given that we don't work for political parties, and that only about 3% of our business is with governments across Canada, we're very independent in terms of what we can poll and report on without fear of backlash or undue influence. These things usually surprise people—our size, our scope of business, and whom we *don't* work for.

Another point that surprises people (especially those who know us personally) is how much education we actually have. Darrell holds a B.A., an M.A., and a Ph.D. in research design. Like him, virtually every aspiring pollster or market researcher needs either an exceptional university track record with a degree related to market research, sociology, or psychology, or at least an impressive set of academic letters after their name. The days are long gone when people who expressed a vague interest in marketing or in people's opinions could start in the telephone calling room and work their way up to a senior research position. Sure, a few exceptions to that rule may still slip by, but those who apply to our company are mostly young, bright, and exceptionally talented people making the brazen claim that they've wanted to work here all their lives. Which, we admit, may be a realistic statement, given that many of them are less than 22 years old and were therefore actually still learning to walk when we were polling on whether Bob Rae was going to be premier of Ontario. (As Ontarians know, before he entered the federal Liberal Party, Mr. Rae did serve as premier of Ontario. Our poll—a poll that, within pundit circles, is still remembered, and that really established our company on the national media scene—was the first to suggest that Bob Rae was on his way to victory over David Peterson.)

Darrell runs the Global Public Affairs division, one of only five über-divisions in an Ipsos mother company that now spans 20 countries. He's also the author of two best-selling books on Canadian public opinion (one is a deadly serious page-turner that he wrote with Ed Greenspon, former editor-in-chief of *The Globe and Mail*, called *Searching for Certainty*; the other one we'll get to a bit later). Prior to joining the Angus Reid Group, Darrell was the director of public opinion research in the office of Canada's prime minister. And before that, Darrell taught at and earned advanced degrees from Wilfrid Laurier University and Carleton University, where he was a Social Science and Humanities Research Council doctoral fellow and the Epstein Scholar. But Darrell—or Dr. Bricker, as his friends call him—is perhaps best known for his commentary on Canadian politics. He has run election polling programs for Canada's major media outlets since 1993, and has appeared as the polling commentator on both CTV's and Global TV's national election-night broadcasts.

Darrell also writes pieces for *The Globe and Mail* and the *National Post,* and he is continually quoted in all of Canada's major news publications, as well as in foreign press from *The New York Times* to *The Economist.* Run an online search on Darrell Bricker and you will see what we're talking about (but ignore the entry about the dressmaker, which has nothing to do with him).

This book's other author is John Wright, chief media spokesperson for Angus/Ipsos Reid since 1989. He often makes the point that with a degree in Tudor-Stuart history and political science, nowadays his original resumé wouldn't get him past the reception desk (okay, he could probably get a job answering the phone). But experience counts for something, because after 20 years of crafting questions and looking at data, he has earned his way to the position of top pollster. Add to this his service as a cabinet minister's assistant, two years in a government-relations position at a huge life insurance company, and five years in the senior ranks of an advertising and communications firm, and it's not a bad track record. He also co-authored and edited the very first public affairs textbook in Canada way back in 1985, and has held leadership, advisory, and board positions in many organizations in both Canada and the United States. He also hosts a weekly show called *Your Opinion Counts* on radio station CRFB and often co-hosts BNN's *Squeeze Play* with Amanda Lang.

And, since the claim behind this book is so bold, we'll list a few facts about Ipsos, headquartered in Paris, France, and publicly traded on the Bourse de Paris (the Paris Stock Exchange). The whole kit and caboodle started out in much the same way its eventual Canadian acquisition did. In 1975, two guys named Didier Truchot and Jean-Marc Lech, with a couple of clients in hand and influenced perhaps by a few bottles of wine, started a company to conduct market research into media-viewing habits. It wasn't long before the businessman and researcher (Truchot) and the brainiac and theoretician (Lech) started to build their client stable, and over the next 34 years they turned it into a global company. A few facts about Ipsos:

- first listed on Paris Stock Exchange (Bourse de Paris): July 1, 1999
- total revenues in 2008: 979.3 million euros ($1,584 million)
- number of countries with Ipsos offices: 64
- number of countries Ipsos does research in: 100+
- number of full-time Ipsos employees: 8,800
- number of clients around the world: 5,000+
- number of interviews conducted each year: 10 million

And our top clients, in alphabetical order:

- Bayer
- Coca-Cola
- Colgate-Palmolive
- Danone
- GlaxoSmithKline
- Kraft
- InBev
- LG Electronics
- Mars (the candy company, not the planet)
- Microsoft

- Nestlé
- Pfizer
- Procter & Gamble
- Reckitt-Benckiser
- S.C. Johnson
- Unilever

We're telling you all of this with one gigantic claim in mind: We Know What You're Thinking. Okay, not in some Orwellian Big Brother way . . . but, actually, yes, close enough. Just think of all the products and services that the companies above provide to consumers like you—from dog food to donuts, from cellphones to candy bars, from macaroni-and-cheese to the beer to wash it down with, to the cleaning materials that clean up the spills and the pill to quell the hangover— we collectively spend millions and millions of hours every year just trying to figure out what people think about, what they do, and what they use, or might want to use, in their day-to-day and long-term lives. The list above contains just a fraction of the household names we work with in this country when examining what Canadians think. When you add to this the banks, insurance companies, restaurants, philanthropic organizations, associations, department stores, sports car manufacturers, hospitals, municipalities, advertising agencies, and media outlets that all want information about Canadians who come from many difference places and speak different languages . . . you can tell that we are very busy folks.

Now, we might know everything there is to know, but there's no way we can put all that down in one book. Actually, we tried a different approach a few years back with another book called *What Canadians Think . . . About Almost Everything*, 33,000 copies of which are out there in people's bathrooms, on bookshelves, perhaps propping up wobbly furniture. What we did then was more akin to packing a book full of facts and figures on opinions that Canadians hold on topic after topic. That book belongs to the line that includes the *Guinness Book of World Records* and *1,001 Fascinating Hockey Stats*—a simple formula and a great one. We made sure it wasn't too heavy, either to hold or to read, but that it would still obligingly offer up a quirky fact when you stuck your finger into it on the subway or in the bath.*

That's what we did with dollops of data from before 2003. But when we figured it was time to write another book, we happened to meet a terrific editor at HarperCollins named Jim Gifford, and when speaking with him and with the very talented Jennifer Lambert at the same address, it took but a nanosecond to understand what could be done with our treasure trove of findings. So we set about creating a book that strikes a balance between telling fun stories about Canadians and teaching new facts about our national character, or rather, our busy mix of many national characters.

But let's also give *hefty* credit where it's due: to our personal *writer-shaper-make-numbers-come-alive-more-human-than-a-pollster* editor, Tom Howell. His work on this manuscript and his vivid sense of humour turned our original tome, *What Canadians Need to Know about the Numbers That We Have Gathered about Their Thoughts and Deeds and Have Interpreted for Their Enjoyment,* with a picture on the front cover of the authors in Speedos walking the red sands of a Prince Edward Island beach, into something much more acceptable for upfront book sales at the mall. We thank him very much for all his talent and fortitude.

---

*Why is it that some book reviewers think a book written by two pollsters has to have at its heart some big, long exposé on what the point is to being Canadian? Honestly, does it always have to be something really profound and include references to Confederation, peace, order and good government, the French/English divide, the First and Second World Wars, immigration and our changing society, or our aging population, wrapped up with allusions to the global recession and our stable banking system? Pleeeaaase, after all these years—since Confederation—of people trying to define this country and its people like some quest for the holy beavertail, we figured there were lots of other texts to choose from and we all deserve a break.

And finally, we'd like to credit HarperCollins production editor Allegra Robinson, who reconfigured the manuscript to make it thoroughly readable, as well as HarperCollins designer Sharon Kish, who ensured the finished book was as good looking as it is fascinating.

POLLS ARE FOR DOGS

While Canada's 13th prime minister may have been the first to say this, we've heard it from many politicians over the years. It ranks right up there with "the only poll that counts is on election day." But why *should* politicians, or anybody else, care about public opinion polls? The reason is that polls do a very good job of predicting what the public is thinking on any day about any topic. In fact, none of the polls we discuss in this book are about how Canadians will vote in the next federal election. But all are as accurate as any election poll that we conduct.

So, how are polls done? There's no magic or black box. The scientific principles are logical and easy to understand. The main idea to get your head around is that you don't have to talk to everybody in Canada to figure out what the nation is thinking. Talking to a sample of Canadians will do the trick. This applies to any survey, whether it's by telephone, on the Internet, by mail, or door to door. The secret is in the sampling.

A proper "random" sample is actually selected carefully, not by some whimsically random behaviour on the part of the pollster. It's a group of Canadians we've picked to represent everybody. For most of the surveys discussed in this book, the group contains roughly 1,000 people.

The key to an accurate survey is how that small group of Canadians is selected. Sampling works this way: Imagine that you have 100 people in a room, and you want to figure out what to order them for lunch. You don't have a clue what to order, but you know that you don't have the luxury of asking them each individually what they would like to eat. And, most importantly, you want to make as many people happy as possible. So you decide to ask a few people in the room to give you input.

You ask everybody to stand up and count off by ones to 10, until each person has a number. Then you write out 10 cards, numbered one to 10, and put them in a hat. You have someone pull a card out of the hat and read you the number. It's three. You then ask all of the 10 people who said "three" what they would like to eat for lunch.* You find out that four people want Chinese food and six want Italian.

So you order 40 Chinese lunches and 60 Italian lunches. To everyone's amazement, the vast majority of the people in the room are thrilled with what you ordered. It was as if you read their minds! Hey, Kreskin, you just did a poll! (By the way, Darrell once followed The Amazing Kreskin as a guest on a TV show, but we digress . . .)

Now, what about that "plus or minus 10%, 19 times out of 20" stuff? What does *that* mean? Let's go back to the lunchroom. If we succeeded in selecting a fair sample by picking all of the number threes, and didn't accidentally select all the vegetarians or low-carb dieters, the rules say we should still expect to be off by a little bit. Not everybody will be satisfied with the lunch order. That's the margin of error. It might turn out that 10 people in the room were stuck with food they didn't really want, which would mean our margin of error was 10%. If we picked another random sample, we shouldn't be surprised if this time five people wanted Chinese food and five wanted Italian. Maybe we should have ordered 50 Chinese lunches and 50 Italian lunches. Great, but even if we had, we shouldn't have expected fewer people to be upset in the end, based on asking a sample of just 10 people and making a prediction about the rest.

The really sad news is that even if we followed all of the rules perfectly and did our lunch poll 20 times, one time we would be wrong by even more than 10%. Maybe that was the unlucky time we happened

---

*A stickler could challenge us at this point. As you might expect, our sampling methods end up being more complicated than this because we have to take into account all the little problems and biases that creep into the sampling process. That's why pollsters such as Darrell need to pour so many years of their life into getting their fancy academic qualifications.

to ask the 10 people who were allergic to pasta. We get used to a margin of error in even the best-performing polls, and over time, we learn to predict what that margin probably is. In most of our polls, we predict a margin of roughly 3%, based on a sample of 1,000 people. That's as well as we can expect our samples to match what's out there in the whole country.

WHO WRITES THE QUESTIONS?!?!

This is probably the most-asked question we get after we explain who we are, what we do, and how we do it. We may have the biggest telephone-interviewing capacity in Canada, with pre-screened online panels made up of hundreds of thousands of people who respond to a survey every six months, and hundreds of thousands of other people whom we reach in different ways for their candid views every year. But as much as we like to boast about those things, the first question we usually get is, "Who writes the questions?" And it's usually asked in some kind of accusatory tone.

So, let's put that question to rest right here at the beginning of the book: We do. There's no kindly old man behind the curtain like in *The Wizard of Oz*, no mysterious black box or cauldron to dip into, and no overbearing evil client fashioned after *Monsters, Inc.* boss Henry J. Waternoose. The boring truth is that everybody who works at our company, on whatever assignment, does their own homework and has access to some of the most experienced question crafters in the land.

And there's an inherent question wrapped up inside of that first one: What keeps pollsters honest, and how can we trust what they say? Well, that's the question that matters the most. You see, we don't have a contract with you. It's not as though you can take us to court if we interpret something in a way that you don't like, and as for the situation when we ask something that you think is so biased you really must phone up the Question & Margin-of-Error Police at the Industry Association who can issue a . . . actually, there is no such thing.

So, we have a few standards that we set for ourselves. Our personal and company integrity comes first. Whatever we do, we have to take responsibility for it, or we won't be in business long or have any kind of reputation that's worth peddling.

We try our best to get at the truth, and if the client or someone else wants to manipulate the results and torture the data to make them lie, then they can go somewhere else and try to get it done there.

At the end of the process—whatever that may be, whether it's the design of a questionnaire, the output, or the interpretation—we reflect on what has transpired and ask ourselves whether this is something that could stand up in court under cross-examination. And when we say "court," we don't mean just the legal stuff; we mean the court of public opinion, where many of our polls show up.

And finally, we realize that when polls are put into the public domain for all to see, we have a special responsibility. Just go to Google and type in either or both of our names with Ipsos and you'll come across thousands and thousands of entries. To us, this is perhaps the most enduring part of our work: capturing what people think at a time in history so that, years from now, when others look back and wonder what Canadians thought or what motivated us as a nation, they can actually find out.

Remember, it wasn't too long ago when if you wanted to find out what people thought during the First World War or at any time right up until the mid-1980s, when polling results started to show up in the Canadian media on a regular basis, you had to find either eyewitnesses or a collection of diaries to substantiate a hypothesis. Researchers would pull up newspapers from the era on microfiche and read the editorials, possibly believing that these reflected the national consensus or popular reaction at the time. Having witnessed polling results representing the views of Canadians from coast to coast that were diametrically opposed to what was written by the publishers and editors of news outlets on many occasions, we'd say it's likely that a vastly more accurate understanding of the Canadian psyche today will be available for future Canadians to draw upon.

And if that wasn't enough to win us posterity, we now work globally—and frequently—with the likes of Reuters News and a host of other clients, which enables us to understand what the people of the planet think about almost everything. So it's been quite a trip for us two pollsters: starting out, seven years before Google existed, when word processors spit out sheets from hooded printers, to today, when we routinely conduct surveys in 23 countries and in almost 100 languages.

There's also one final element that we never forget: Polls are a snapshot, and people can change their minds. Many pundits have unfortunately elevated the status of our market research expertise to a level of clairvoyance. Well, it's not. But, given our experience and the longevity of tracking data, we feel comfortable saying that nobody's completely unpredictable. We pretty well know which sorts of people out there have the propensity to change their minds—and why. So, let's dive into the facts and help you get to know yourself and others in this great country of ours. And, of course, we know you'll like it.

PART ONE / WHERE DO YOU BELONG?

When it comes to choosing where to live, we often find our hands are tied. It may be because of family obligations, or the requirements of a job, or any of a million other reasons. But imagine that you were completely free to live anywhere in Canada, and that someone handed you a bunch of brochures in which each region tried its best to entice you. The brochure from British Columbia would probably be full of pictures of mountains and healthy-looking people jogging by the sea; Alberta's might advertise economic opportunities, along with a few dinosaur bones (and maybe a beach from a place called Northumberland); Saskatchewan and Manitoba could perhaps team up to sell you on Prairie life with pictures of canola fields and old sheds leaning away from the wind; Ontario might throw in a free CD featuring a toe-tapping musical anthem based on its slogan "There's No Place Like This"; Quebec could shill its historical buildings and autumnal forests; and finally, Atlantic Canada would arrange a photographic collage of lobsters, fiddle-players, and a moored boat or two. All attractive in their own way, but not much to go on.*

The problem with all these brochures, apart from their clichés, is that, even after bombarding you with impassioned arguments, none of them would tell you what you really need to know: "Where can I

---

*Leafing back through the pile again, it unfortunately seems that the brochures from Canada's north must have got stuck in the mail. We aren't giving a profile of the northern territories of Canada in this section of the book because national polling rarely includes Yukon, the Northwest Territories, or Nunavut—or, more accurately, these populations *are* polled but the sample sizes are too small for us to isolate particular facts about these areas.

find people who are going to agree with me?" After all, one of the great comforts in life is being surrounded by like-minded people who don't raise pesky objections every time we voice an opinion. (You might not agree with this, of course—you might be the sort of person who's always looking for an argument, in which case you'd be happiest living in a place where most people share that desire! We suggest Quebec or the Atlantic provinces, where half the population likes to argue so much that they'll take issue with you for the fun of it, even when they broadly agree with what you're saying.)

Part One of this book gives you the answer that's missing from the brochures. It picks out the part of Canada where you're most likely to fit in. So, leave aside the pretty pictures of boats, dinosaurs, farmhouses, and mountains, and answer the following questions:

- What would you rather put your hand on: the top of an Egyptian pyramid or the Holy Grail?
- What do you think of the one-cent coin—isn't it completely pointless?
- When it comes to politics, what would you rather have: a good standard of debate among your friends and family, or a good standard of debate among politicians?
- Do you want to renovate your kitchen?
- Let's say you have enough money to retire. Would you rather continue working anyway?
- The singer Jon Bon Jovi has asked you to accompany him to a glitzy movie premiere. Are you interested in going?
- Actress Julia Roberts wants you to come with her to a glitzy movie premiere, but if you'd rather take your mom instead, Julia will understand. Whom do you choose?
- How many books have you read in the past year?

- How long do you spend in the shower?
- Do you think your local government should provide financial support for the arts?

Part Two of the book then gets into lots of fun topics about different groupings of Canadians. Part Three features *The Great Canadian Quiz*, and we know you will want to impress your friends with your great results.

But first, we've come up with some new ideas for what provincial brochures *should* say. Help yourself to a coffee, and take a look . . .

1 / THE BRITISH COLUMBIAN

This is the place for local arts and culture. People agree emphatically that funding for the arts should not be left up to private businesses and foundations, but should get a boost from local governments. Ninety-one percent of B.C. residents praise the selection of events and activities in their community, and it's the only region of Canada where there's complete agreement with the idea that a vibrant cultural scene is great for the local economy. British Columbians are significantly more confident than other Canadians that their local arts scenes attract tourists.

"I strongly agree that our arts scene attracts tourists to the area."

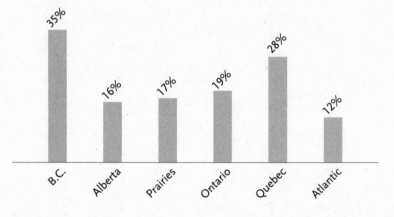

A further 53% of British Columbians say they "somewhat" agree that the local arts scene is vibrant, attractive, and good for tourism. If you add the "somewhat" people to the "strongly" people, you get a huge group—nine out of ten people in the province—signing their names in the "agree" column. Spend public money on the arts, get money back from tourists, and enjoy a better economy overall: In the world of opinion polls, nine out of ten counts as resounding support for this concept.

Oh, and if you're intrigued by the Egyptian pyramids, you'd fit right in here. British Columbians were given the following list of options for things they could touch:

- the Holy Grail
- the Stanley Cup
- the Hope Diamond
- the very top of an Egyptian pyramid
- an Academy Award (i.e., an Oscar)
- Dorothy's ruby slippers from *The Wizard of Oz*

Roughly half of them chose the pyramid. Perhaps, on a symbolic level, this suggests that British Columbians share a lust for travel and history rather than for religion, sports, wealth, fame, or . . . well, whatever those ruby slippers represent. As a matter of fact, if you're inclined towards Dorothy's slippers, then sorry, you'll stick out in B.C. because hardly anyone chose that option. Better try your luck in Saskatchewan or Manitoba.

"I'd rather touch Dorothy's ruby slippers."

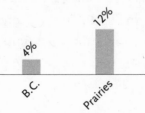

4% B.C. 12% Prairies

Although still a minority in their provinces, people who want to touch Dorothy's ruby slippers are three times more common in Saskatchewan and Manitoba than in B.C. In *The Wizard of Oz*, Dorothy's ruby slippers whisk her back home to Kansas, where much of the landscape, as in parts of Saskatchewan and Manitoba, is completely flat. Coincidence? Quite possibly.

MYTH-BUSTING: ECO-FRIENDLY BRITISH COLUMBIA

Here's a stereotype you may have encountered: the west-coast hippie who wears socks with sandals, an eco-friendly hemp T-shirt, and a button for the Green Party. Forty percent of Canadians pick B.C. as the most environmentally conscious province in the country, well ahead of nearest rivals Ontario and Quebec, which win 10% each in this vote, thanks mostly to the opinions of their own large populations. Well, let's take a moment to dispel the idea that British Columbia is full of eco-fiends.

It's true that the Lower Mainland areas are literally green—the city of Vancouver receives 1,219 mm of rain every year (compared to 265 mm in Saskatoon)—but that doesn't necessarily lead to greener attitudes. Adults in B.C. are *less likely* to see themselves as having a strong personal responsibility for the province's environmental health and are *no better than average* when it comes to reducing consumption and using cloth shopping bags rather than plastic ones. Asked to grade their own individual performances in taking actions that preserve and protect the environment, most give themselves a B or a C. Their concerns lead them to recycle or compost but usually don't have a "very significant" impact on the cars they drive, the food they buy, the detergents they use, or their principal mode of transportation.

We asked British Columbians how their environmental concerns affect their actions. Here's how many told us their concerns had a "very significant impact" on . . .

- the car they drive: 21%
- the food they buy: 19%
- the detergent or cleaning products they use: 27%
- their waste management practices (recycling, composting): 56%
- their principal mode of transportation: 24%

Thanks to the abundant local water supplies in parts of the province, British Columbians have become the most garden hose–happy people in Canada. British Columbians sprinkle their lawns an average of twice a week throughout the summer—and remember, that's just the *average*. If you're the sort of person who wants to water your lawn three times a week in the high, dry summer of late July, well, you'll be in much better company here in B.C. than, say, in Alberta . . .

"I water my lawn 2–3 times a week all through the summer."

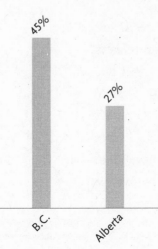

Before any Albertans get the idea that they're the great water conservers, remember that question about the shower on page 19? Turns out Albertans like to let the water run. If, on a typical morning, an average British Columbian and an average Albertan wake up simultaneously, roll out of bed, shuffle off to the bathroom, and turn on the shower at exactly the same moment, the British Columbian will be reaching for the towel precisely 1 minute and 18 seconds before the Albertan.*

Then there's litter. Teenagers in B.C. are the *least likely* to do anything if they see a stranger toss a gum wrapper on the ground in front of them. It might be because of a larger character trait in this province: the relaxed attitude. When asked to define themselves as either "green fiends," "environmentally laid-back," or "cynics," the teens here overwhelmingly choose "laid-back."

Given that today's teens are tomorrow's opinion-makers, check out where the green tide is really coming from. Despite the "green" image of Canada's west coast, teenagers in Prince Edward Island are more than twice as likely to call themselves

"How I define myself environmentally"

- green fiend: 15%
- laid-back: 78%
- cynic: 7%

---

*The disclaimer here is that these two people must be *extremely average*, which is paradoxically a rare thing. But the point is: overall, we know that Albertans spend an average of 8.4 minutes in the shower, compared to 7.1 minutes for British Columbians.

"green fiends" who recycle everything, conserve energy when possible, and encourage those around them to respect the environment.

"I am a green fiend!"

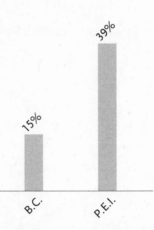

A majority of residents in the small city of Nanaimo, on Vancouver Island, are seriously concerned about the danger that lawn pesticides pose to cats and dogs. About 60% of the local people feel very strongly about this.

This is at odds with the small city of Abbotsford, on the Lower Mainland, where only a minority, 40%, are equally concerned.

British Columbia boasts a wide variety of landscapes, from the soggy delta to the sandy Okanagan, from deep valleys to high plateaus. Such a mix of landscapes affects how "eco" people are in the garden. Some British Columbians are hyper-vigilant about avoiding chemical pesticides, for instance. In other parts of the province, gardeners sprinkle these chemicals liberally. Depending on whether you prefer green politics or green leaves, different towns in B.C. might appeal to you more. If you don't want to live next door to someone who uses pesticides (and then maybe waters that lawn three times a week so the chemicals run off onto your grass!), here's some useful information on how B.C. communities stack up against each other.

"We put pesticides on our lawn or garden in the last 12 months."

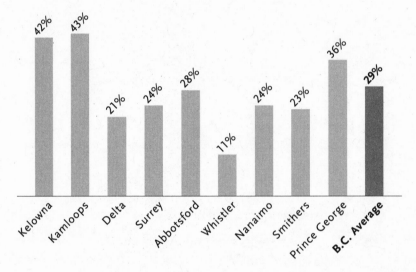

Finally, regarding that socks-with-sandals trend mentioned earlier, we've got one word for you: don't.* Seven in 10 British Columbians give this fashion statement the thumbs-down. (Interestingly, the most emphatic group on this issue are women between the ages of 35 and 54. Perhaps they're the most commonly exposed to socks-and-sandals wearers?) Overall, it's a bigger social no-no than guys who wear Speedos at the beach.

---

*Some people may argue that *don't* is technically two words. If you're one of these people, go take a look at the statistics related to argumentativeness on page 60—they'll probably be right up your alley.

"I live in B.C. and I give this fashion choice a thumbs-down."

Bookworms

The British Columbian has read more books than any other Canadian in the past year, but the reading list probably did not include the Bible. The only province with *less* Bible reading is Quebec (not counting Catholic priests). Instead, B.C. readers prefer other sorts of books, particularly mysteries, such as detective fiction and thrillers. If you put aside all the people who don't read books at all (because you obviously aren't one of them!), the typical B.C. reader goes through 33 books a year.

How many books did you read last year?

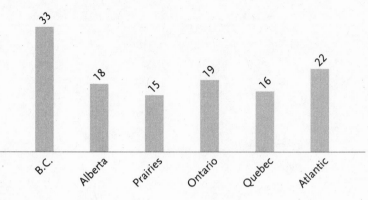

33   18   15   19   16   22

B.C.   Alberta   Prairies   Ontario   Quebec   Atlantic

The places where people read the most books—B.C. and the Atlantic provinces—are the closest to the ocean.

The provinces where people read the fewest books—Manitoba and Saskatchewan—are farthest from the ocean.

Meaningless coincidence? Quite possibly.

A word of warning: Six out of every ten British Columbians want to get rid of the one-cent coin. If you feel affection for this useless piece of metal, we're afraid you'll be in the minority here.

WHAT MAKES BRITISH COLUMBIANS UNIQUE

We've selected some prominent points that help define those who live on the "wet coast." If you hail from the province of British Columbia, compared to your fellow Canadians, you are . . .

- *least likely to strongly agree that your eating habits could use some improvement.*

- least likely to use your mobile device for phone calls and most likely to use it to share content such as photos, video, e-mails, and text messages, or to search and browse the Internet.
- most likely to answer your mobile device if it rings in the middle of making love.
- most likely to have received a dog free from someone who was giving it away to a good home.
- most likely to have got your pet cat spayed or neutered, and most likely to have got it tattooed.
- least likely to agree that it's okay for drivers to talk on a cellphone while driving.
- most likely to indicate that your work experience is much better than you expected it would be.
- most likely to be worried about your home being burglarized.
- least likely to have had a practice drill of your family's fire-escape plan (if you have one).
- least likely, on a typical weekday, to use text messaging for social, non-business communication, but most likely to use regular mail to communicate with friends.
- most likely to use an instant messaging program, such as MSN Messenger, for social, non-business communication, but most likely to feel more connected to another person face to face rather than when they're on the other end of some electronic technology.
- most likely to say that a few times a year you have ruined a piece of clothing because you weren't sure how to properly wash or care for it, but also most likely to keep all of your laundry supplies stocked (correlation?).
- most likely, if you could possess a supernatural power, to choose the ability to read other people's minds.

2 / THE ALBERTAN

Albertans say keep the penny, and get rid of the rules against paying for private health care. According to their own testimony, they're the most right-wing people in Canada, and 32% of other Canadians agree (the nearest rival is Ontario, chosen by 22% of non-Ontarians). Predictably enough, many Albertans think the Canadian news media are "too liberal," a belief that's twice as common here as in British Columbia and Quebec, where more people criticize the media for being too conservative. What might be harder to fit into this, and other rather unfair stereotyping, is that Albertans are also the most involved in fighting HIV/AIDS in developing countries, the most inclined to answer "human rights" when asked for the key issues facing world leaders, and the least likely to agree that Canada would be better off if immigrants went back where they came from.

In Canada, more people want immigrants to "go back where they came from" than place human rights at the top of the list of priorities for world leaders. One regional exception to this is the province of Alberta.*

---

*After the First World War, Walter Wright, a sergeant major of the British West Yorkshire Regiment and a veteran of the Somme who was wounded badly at the counterattack at DeVille Wood, crossed the ocean in 1920 and arrived in Edmonton's "Shantytown" to settle. While there, he enlisted in the Edmonton Battalion, became involved in founding Canada's national rugby team, and, with his wife, Mary, produced a son named William, who begat one of this book's co-authors, who believes that Alberta's acceptance of immigrants to Canada is genetically embedded.

Boomers on the Move

Alberta's next generation of retirees—Baby Boomers currently between the ages of 48 and 52—are planning to move when they retire in order to find somewhere with a better climate or cheaper housing. Okay, not *every single retiree* is going to move, but a clear majority of them (56%) will. Only a third of Ontario Boomers and a quarter of Atlantic Boomers would move for a better climate. (The proportion who'd move for financial reasons is slightly higher but not much.) When asked for the most important feature of a retirement home or community, 92% of Albertans chose a place close to nature. If you're a retiring Boomer looking to live in a condo community where everything is maintained, with security and landscaping, plus a pool and a golf course, Albertans may be your sort of people. Three-quarters of Boomers here find that idea appealing, compared to just half of their contemporaries in B.C.

Movie Dates

Sometimes we find ourselves asking strange and hypothetical questions, like the time a television company wanted to know which celebrities people would want to take to a movie premiere. Here were the options given to men across the country:

- your mother
- Angelina Jolie
- Julia Roberts
- Hillary Clinton
- Condoleezza Rice
- Britney Spears
- Paris Hilton
- (don't know)

Alberta is the only province where a clear majority of men chose their mom. None of the men in the sample chose Hillary Clinton. One in ten didn't know who to pick.

"I'd take my mom rather than any of the celebrities on the list."

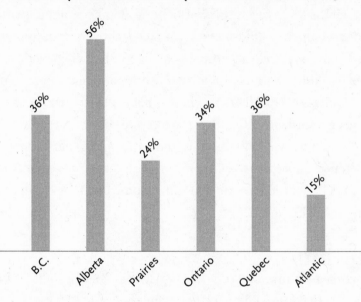

Here were the options given to women:

- your father
- George Clooney
- Brad Pitt
- Al Gore
- Stephen Harper
- Jon Bon Jovi
- Tom Cochrane
- (don't know)

Women didn't give such a clear vote of confidence to their dads, although Alberta gals were again the most loyal to their parents (41%

chose their dad). The other popular answers were George Clooney and Stephen Harper. The least popular was actor and singer Jon Bon Jovi, who unfortunately ranked beneath "Don't know."

> **We asked women whom they'd take to a glitzy movie premiere. Alberta is the only province where nobody chose Jon Bon Jovi.**

WHERE ALBERTANS LEAD THE COUNTRY

Albertans are the most likely to admit to getting tongue-tied when trying to convey their feelings, and the most likely to say that their romantic relationship resembles that of a certain semi-homegrown prime minister* and his wife. Men in Alberta are the most inclined to say that a woman is the boss of their household. People in this province are particularly likely to think that disgraced media baron Conrad Black was given too lenient a sentence after he was found guilty of fraud in 2007. They're the most likely to believe Canadians should not hold dual citizenship. They're the most concerned about online sexual predators, and this is where the largest proportion of parents have put controls on their Internet browser to prevent their children from visiting unsuitable websites. Albertans are the most likely to skip a meal, the most inclined to have an afternoon snack, the most keen to renovate their deck or patio, and the most strongly opposed to marriage between same-sex couples. They're the most inclined to read non-fiction history books, the most pleased with the quality of local museums and libraries, and the most likely to believe there's a ghost living in their house.

---

*The authors would like to personally and vigorously repudiate any implication that Canada's 22nd prime minister and his wife are anything but first among equals when it comes to our country's most romantically inclined couples. On top of that, she has a very hot motorcycle and he, well, got himself a pretty cool job.

WHERE ALBERTANS TRAIL BEHIND

Proportionally speaking, Alberta is the province where the fewest people sleep naked.

"I like sleeping naked."

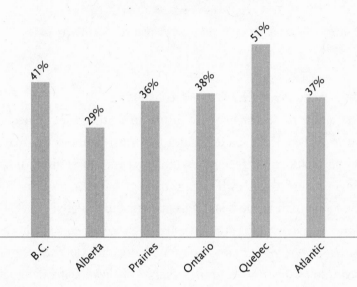

Albertans are also the least willing to pay more up front for "green" home building products, the least pleased with the condition of local schools (72% are displeased), and the least inclined to legalize euthanasia (although there's still a slim majority in favour of legalizing it).

AND ABOUT THAT STAMPEDE . . .

If you live in Alberta and don't want to go against the flow, you need to join the three-quarters of the population that looks forward to the Calgary Stampede every year. A clear majority of Albertans see it as much more than a ten-day party, so to fit in with the general opinion, it's best to refer to it as one of the most important "cultural" events in the province.

What Makes Albertans Unique

If you're from Alberta, then compared to other Canadians, you are . . .

- *most likely to agree that it's more important for the Canadian government to focus on jobs than climate change at the moment.*
- *most likely to consider taking a cruise for your next vacation.*
- *most likely to agree that cruise ships are a romantic place to take a vacation (A tie with Quebec—ooh-la-la!)*
- *most likely of those aged 50 and up to agree that your retirement date has been delayed because of the 2008–2009 recession.*
- *most likely to strongly agree that laughter is one of the world's greatest aphrodisiacs. (Ha ha ha! A tie with Ontario!)*
- *most likely to strongly agree that you know how to change a diaper (if you're a father expecting your first child).*
- *least likely to agree that Canada should take serious action on climate change right now even if it means higher deficits.*
- *least likely to agree that development of the Alberta tar sands should stop until a clean method of extraction can be found.*
- *least likely to agree that the Canadian government should adopt only economic stimulus measures that are environmentally sustainable.*
- *least likely to strongly agree that you are doing your fair share to fight climate change.*
- *least likely to say you think you're doing "more than most people" when it comes to helping the environment.*
- *least likely to agree that your eating habits will help you live a long and healthy life.*
- *least likely to agree that you've made a concerted effort to cut junk food from your diet. (Hey, pass the chips: tied with Ontario.)*
- *most likely to let your laundry pile up until you have no clean underwear.*
- *least likely to agree that you are currently in a relationship.*

- *most likely to retrieve your mobile device if it falls in a pile of doggie doo-doo.*
- *most likely to buy a cat from a pet store.*
- *most likely to have got your cat licensed and microchipped.*
- *most likely to feel your employer works hard to cultivate a positive working culture; most likely to say that your workplace atmosphere inspires you to work efficiently and productively; and least likely to say that you're dragged down by a negative atmosphere at work.*
- *most likely to use social networking websites such as Facebook or MySpace on a typical weekday for social, non-business communication.*
- *most likely to choose the ability to fly if you were able to choose a supernatural power. (Take off, eh!)*
- *more likely than any other Canadian to be envious of a friend or neighbour's laundry room.*

3 / THE PRAIRIE CANADIAN

Okay, let's deal with this "Man/Sask" polling issue right up front. This is the thing that our Prairie cousins hate the most when we do our research for the news media: They get lumped together in the results when they are, in fact, two separate provinces.

Imagine how you would feel if you lived on the planet Hoth in the fictional universe of Star Wars (where Hoth is the sixth planet of a remote system of the same name). Yours is a world covered in snow and ice, with numerous moons, pelted by meteorites from a nearby asteroid belt, and with native creatures that include the Wampa and the Tauntun. But some intergalactic research company has lumped you in with Sirius—the brightest star in the heavens, visible to all of us earthling Canadians and known colloquially as the Dog Star due to its prominence in its constellation, Canis Major (English: *Big Dog*)—with the result that your culture always refers to the two of you as "Hot/Dog." Every time you saw, read, or heard this, it would be like a big kick in the astronomy, right?

Well, let's assure you, we don't do this to slight Saskatchewaners and Manitobans. If you read this book's introduction (our statistics show that most readers sometimes or usually skip prefaces and intro materials, and dive straight into the meaty part of books), then you'll know that a random, proportionate poll is based on how many people live in an area—the more people you poll, the lower the margin of error. At the same time, the more people you poll, the more it costs to do the work. Not everybody can afford to do, say, 500 interviews per province, which would be a pretty good sample size, because that would mean that for 10 provinces we would be doing 5,000 interviews.

Every completed 20-minute interview costs roughly $54, putting the cost of this big poll at $270,000. Even for a rich company, that's a lot of money. Most of the time, they want to take the pulse of the country for a more reasonable price.

What we have found over the last many decades is that if you do a survey of 1,000 people randomly chosen, but drawn so as to reflect how the country is populated, then you end up with pretty accurate results (the figures we end up with are within about 3% of the true figure, 19 times out of 20). But to get this level of accuracy, we have to amalgamate some parts of the country—Atlantic Canada gets mushed together, as do Manitoba and Saskatchewan—to bump up the size of the population groups we're trying to reflect. We can be fairly confident basing our research on what 140 Prairie Canadians say about their region, where 2 million people live. But when you split that group in half, then a few off-the-wall responses are more likely to wreck the data. That means it's more iffy to draw detailed conclusions from what 70 Saskatchewaners say about their province, where 1 million people live.

We have a thing called an "omnibus poll" that surveys just 1,000 people across the country. People or companies can buy one question at a time, at a price ranging from about $1,300 to $1,700, depending on the length of the question. It's a good, cheap, and fast poll—exactly the type that the media like to buy, because then they can do more of them and save their money. Clients who want to get closer to you and your home will spend the big bucks for much larger samples of people in the provinces, to the point where they can learn things about just the people who live in Saskatchewan, or even just the people who live in Prince Albert.

That's it. The "Man/Sask" thing (and the same goes for Atlantic Canada) really has to do with how many people live in an area and how much it costs to ask enough people to get a read on what they think. When we survey 1,000 people proportionately across the country, these great—but also small—provinces end up with really tiny numbers of people in the survey, so we have to mush them together in order to get readable results.

Okay. Money talks, as it always does. But someone from Manitoba might still pipe up with an objection: "That's not only unfair, it's inaccurate, because it really distorts reality. Our two provinces are just so different from each other." Hmm . . . Well, we have some information about that, too.

On a few points, people who live in Winnipeg think very differently from people who live in Saskatoon. But these points tend to be local and distinct to each community as opposed to the province as a whole. At a provincial level, when we pull in big samples and split out Manitoba from Saskatchewan, we keep seeing a lot of common ground on politics, big issues, and consumer habits.

	Sask. (%)	Man. (%)
Voted with their local candidate in mind	22	25
Voted based on the party leader	21	21
Voted because of how the parties stand on the issues	55	53

We asked voters in the two provinces which leader and which party in 2008 would do the best job of providing a government that is "closest to my personal views."

	Sask. (%)	Man. (%)
Stephen Harper/Conservatives	44	40
Stephane Dion/Liberals	13	17
Jack Layton/NDP	25	23
Elizabeth May/Green Party	4	6

Which leader and which party would do the best job of fixing our health care system?

	Sask. (%)	Man. (%)
Stephen Harper/Conservatives	30	28
Stephane Dion/Liberals	10	12
Jack Layton/NDP	37	37
Elizabeth May/Green Party	2	3

Which leader and which party would do the best job of managing moral issues like same-sex marriage and abortion?

	Sask. (%)	Man. (%)
Stephen Harper/Conservatives	29	28
Stephane Dion/Liberals	14	17
Jack Layton/NDP	22	16
Elizabeth May/Green Party	3	5

Prairie citizens attended church, or other religious services or meetings, in the past year

	Sask. (%)	Man. (%)
more than once a week	5	6
once a week	11	11
a few times a month	7	8
once a month	3	4
a few times a year	15	17
at least once a year	9	9
not at all	46	41

Here are the numbers for the those who agreed with the statement:

	Sask. (%)	Man. (%)
my religious beliefs are important in deciding how I cast my vote	17	16

Okay, there were a few points of diversion. Look at how many people agreed with these statements:

	Sask. (%)	Man. (%)
It would be better in the long run if Quebec were to separate from the rest of Canada	28	19
I've got a gun	30	19
I drink wine	39	49
I use hairstyling gel	35	29
I use hairstyling mousse	27	22

(By the way, the number for Newfoundland and Labrador: 32%)

So, you see what we see: two geographically distinct provinces with occasionally divergent views but, for the most part, folks who are pretty similar (except with respect to hair care products—no doubt used in Saskatchewan to protect the 'do when the prairie wind blows across the wheat fields). Now that we've got through that, let's use a kinder, gentler way to describe "Man/Sask" residents: *Prairie Canadians*. So, pray tell, what are these folks like?

Well, if you're the hard-working sort, you'll find kindred spirits in this part of the country. Roughly half of these people would continue working even if they had the money to retire.

"I'd keep on working anyway."

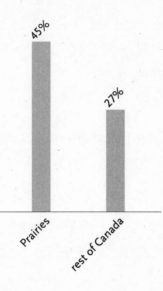

Most of those approaching retirement would like to find a water-front to live near, although this is a much lower priority here than in the rest of the country. Those still working are content to stay put and wouldn't move to Alberta even for a higher-paying job. (Only one in six would take such an offer, compared to one out of three Ontarians.)

NO SEX PLEASE, WE'RE FROM THE LITTLE HOUSE ON THE PRAIRIE . . .
It is fairly unlikely that a randomly chosen resident of Saskatchewan or Manitoba wants more sex. Only 32% say they do. (Overall, half of Canadians say they want more.)

If you want a good standard of political debate, it's worth noting that half of Prairie residents consider the political class to be good debaters. That's a much bigger proportion than in the rest of the country. In Alberta, for instance, just a quarter of the people pay politicians the same compliment. And if you prefer frivolous debates to political ones, and would love an evening of frivolity with the actress Julia Roberts, well, moving to the Prairies won't make it any more likely to happen, but at least you'll easily find sympathy among the 31% of men here who share the dream. They pick Julia as their ideal date for a night at the movies. (Among women, it's a toss-up between Dad and George Clooney.)

There's something else we need to settle here. Earlier in this section of the book, a poll flattered residents of British Columbia by suggesting that they're the biggest bookworms in the country. It's true that B.C.'s readers apparently have ravenous appetites, particularly for mysteries and thrillers, which are less popular in Saskatchewan and Manitoba. But when it comes to being Canada's top readers, Prairie Canadians can certainly rival the British Columbian claim to that title. In fact, here's the "top readers" table for the whole country to put it all in perspective:

"Yes, I've read at least one book in the last year."

Saskatchewan and Manitoba	78%
B.C.	76%
Alberta	71%
Ontario	69%
Atlantic provinces	66%
Quebec	62%

THE TOP THREE PRAIRIE QUIRKS

It's an affectionate belief in much of the country that people who spend their lives on the Prairies tend to become, well, a little quirky. Here are a few bits of evidence in support of that prejudice.

The Prairie Canadian believes in the supernatural.

The name Manitoba is related to the word *manitou*, referring to a supernatural spirit, hence the provincial slogan, "Spirited Energy." Turns out that people in this part of the country take these words literally.

Overall, most Canadians don't believe in ghosts. But in Saskatchewan and Manitoba, most say they do.

And when it comes to supernatural winged agents of Heaven, the answer is even more emphatic, although we asked a follow-up question here, and found out that only a quarter of Prairie people consider an angel to be a paranormal creature who lives in Heaven and resembles a human being but has a pair of wings as well as arms. Half the respondents clarified that they prefer to define an angel as a regular human being who is either particularly good-hearted or chosen by God to perform a certain role.

"I believe in spirits and ghosts."

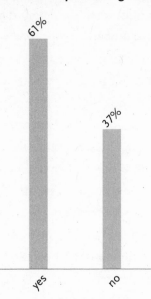

"I believe in angels."

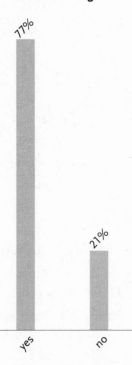

The Prairie Canadian loves coupons.

The Prairies are home to the most ardent collectors of coupons. Three-quarters of respondents here say they go through newspaper ads looking for sales and keep inserts and flyers for days to reread what's being offered.

The Prairie Canadian has an immigration complex.

Wait, no. We mean that the Prairie responses to questions about immigrants are particularly *complex*. On the one hand, people in Saskatchewan and Manitoba are the most likely to get angry when recent immigrants demand the same rights as Canadian citizens. One-quarter of the Prairie population, a much bigger group than in Alberta, believes that immigrants take too many jobs away from Canadians.

"Immigrants take too many jobs away from Canadians."

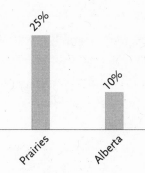

On the other hand, agreement with the statement "Canada is not taking in enough immigrants" was higher in the Prairies than anywhere else in the country.

"Canada is not taking in enough immigrants."

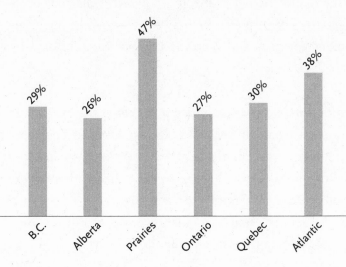

WHAT MAKES PRAIRIE CANADIANS UNIQUE

If you're a Prairie Canadian, you are . . .

- *most likely to agree that your eating habits need a lot of improvement.*
- *most likely to worry that you might get seasick on a cruise ship.*
- *most likely to agree that you are currently in a relationship.*
- *most likely to strongly agree that laughter is an important element in keeping sex and romance alive.*
- *most likely to say that you let your clothes sit in the washer for days before putting them in the dryer, or let them sit in the dryer for days before folding.*
- *least likely to agree that under President Obama the United States will do more to tackle climate change than Canada will.*
- *least likely to strongly agree that you spend a lot of time trying to improve your eating habits.*
- *least likely to agree that cruise ships are a romantic place to take a vacation. (Could be related to that "seasick" thing above.)*

- least likely to secretly hope that your lover will "spice it up" for Valentine's Day.
- least likely to purchase a product or a gift prompted by the knowledge that a portion of the sale will go to supporting a charitable cause.
- most likely to have secretly used your mobile device in the bathroom.
- most likely in the country to fish your mobile device out of the toilet if it falls in, and also most likely to sort through a garbage can for your mobile device if you think it has fallen in.
- most likely to have received your cat from a friend or relative.
- most likely to say that your experience at work is worse than you expected.
- most likely to say that you hate your workplace culture and don't fit in well at all.
- most likely to choose the ability to time travel (if you were able to choose a supernatural power—but you are the only group that tries to choose two superpowers, and the most likely to choose the ability to steal another person's powers).
- most likely to rank "outdoor maintenance or gardening" as your favourite household chore.
- most likely to be fairly content with issues of importance to the country because they really don't affect you or matter that much to you.

AND FINALLY

People from Saskatchewan and Manitoba want to keep the one-cent coin. They're confident in Canada's water supply. They're more likely than Ontarians to skip breakfast, but less likely to skip lunch. Fewer afternoon snacks are consumed here than anywhere else in Canada. Prairie citizens shower for exactly the same length of time as British Columbians. In the summer, they water their lawns once a week or not at all.

4 / THE ONTARIAN

Ontario, home to Canada's national parliament as well as the country's largest city, thinks of itself as "Central Canada," and indeed, when it comes to opinion polls, this province has an extraordinary gift for finding the middle of the pack. This makes it hard to point out a whole bunch of provincial quirks or extremes. What's extreme about Ontario is its *middleness*.

Indeed, Premier William G. Davis (also known to some as "Brampton Billy"), who governed the province from 1971 to 1985, attributed his success to his "bland" policies and politics.

It seems that the 18th premier of the province actually spoke the truth. Here's just a brief list of habits and traits for which the Ontario numbers are extremely *average* compared to Canada's other provinces and regions:

- reading the Bible
- believing in angels
- going out on New Year's Eve
- wanting to touch the Holy Grail
- wanting local government to give more support to the arts
- being interested in undergoing plastic surgery
- reading books
- reading cookbooks*

---

*Oh, okay. To be honest, the number of respondents in our reading survey who checked "cookbooks" as part of their reading list was so small that we can't rely on them to give us the correct proportions. As a point of interest, however, even in this statistically unreliable data field, Ontarians manage to occupy the middle.

- planning to renovate in the next two years
- sleeping naked
- wanting to take Brad Pitt or Angelina Jolie to a movie premiere
- claiming to be the boss of the household
- believing in (and approving of) Santa Claus
- rating the standard of political debate
- choosing to continue to work even if given enough money to retire

... and so on. To find Ontario edging cautiously away from the national mean, you need to address Canadian nationalism itself. We asked people to consider their feelings of loyalty and decide whether they belonged first and foremost to their locality or town, to their province or region, to their country, to North America, or to the whole world. Most Ontarians say "my country."

"I belong first and foremost to my country."

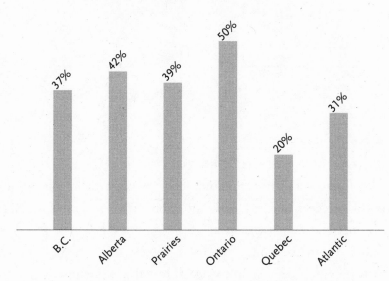

Ontarians are also the most likely to feel a strong attachment to the beaver and the maple leaf as national symbols, and to say it's really important for high school students to study national history.

"I strongly believe that high school students
must learn Canadian history in order to graduate."

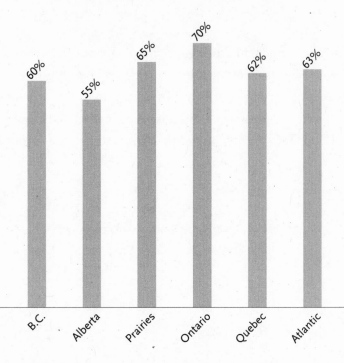

WHEN ONTARIANS FEEL STRONGLY

Middle-of-the-road results from opinion polls don't mean that Ontario is full of people who can't make up their mindsor who don't have strong opinions. When it comes to the big issues, people in this province are loath to choose the response "Don't know." If you come to Ontario, expect to meet people who express the following opinions:

I won't date a smoker.
Sixty percent of single Ontarians would refuse to date someone who smokes.

I strongly approve of my community's overall "character."
Ninety-two percent of Ontarians approve of the character of their local community; most emphasize that it's "very good." They say they almost always encounter the qualities of respect, responsibility, and honesty in their fellow citizens.

I want Canada to be active in world affairs.
Very few Ontarians (4%) disagree with this.

I want Alberta to share its oil wealth.
Six in ten Ontarians think oil sands revenues should benefit all of Canada.

I think cigarette manufacturers deceived the public.
Seven in ten Ontarians believe cigarette-makers deliberately lied to the public about the health problems caused by smoking, and want governments to sue the tobacco industry to recover health care costs.

I want to ban smoking in cars when kids are in the back seat. (This became a provincial law in 2009.)
The typical Ontarian does not believe that parents have the right to smoke cigarettes in their own cars while children are present. This is a public health decision, people say, not a parenting choice.

I listen to other people's conversation while waiting in a lineup.
Eighty-two percent of Ontarians admit to eavesdropping. We include this fact not because people feel so strongly about eavesdropping, but

because we think it's something to bear in mind when expressing your own strong opinions in a public place.

EXCEPTIONS TO THE RULE

Occasionally, Ontario breaks its usual habit of being squarely in the middle of Canada. The province manages to lead, for instance, in wanting to give charitable donations rather than physical gifts—that's the fundraising scheme in which charities suggest we avoid wasting money on a birthday item for a friend who doesn't really need anything and instead send the equivalent sum to a good cause in our friend's name. Roughly half of Ontario residents have done this, well ahead of the national average of 37%.

Other Ontario exceptions don't score as many points for high-mindedness or even significance. Ontarians are the most likely to have a bedtime snack. They're the most inclined to use a concentrated liquid detergent in their washing machines. They skip break-fast approximately once a week. And so on.

WHAT MAKES ONTARIANS UNIQUE

Here's a list of other Ontarian highlights and lowlights that jumped out at us. Compared to other Canadians, if you're from Ontario, you are . . .

- *most likely to strongly agree that laughter is one of the world's greatest aphrodisiacs. (Okay, this was a tie with Alberta . . . get together and humour yourselves!)*
- *most likely to say that a shared sense of humour is very important when it comes to sex and romance.*
- *least likely to agree that your eating habits need a lot of improvement.*
- *least likely to agree that you have made a concerted effort to cut out junk food. (Okay, another tie with Alberta . . . and remember, chocolate is an aphrodisiac!)*

- most likely, if you had $10,000 to spend, to buy new home appliances.
- least likely to strongly agree that you know how to change a diaper (if you're a father expecting your first child). (Okay, this was a tie with Atlantic Canada dads-to-be . . . time to do a "webinar"!)
- most likely to find yourself able to do the type of work you best enjoy (if you're a small-business owner).
- most likely to have secretly used your mobile device at a funeral, but least likely to use your hand to fish your mobile device out of a toilet if it falls in.
- most likely not to get passionate or protest about an issue, believing there's no sense making any noise because nothing ever happens as a result.
- most likely to be fairly content with the levels of crime in your neighbourhood because it doesn't really affect you personally or matter that much to you. (Tell that to people in Toronto!)
- most likely to adopt a stray cat, most likely to buy a dog from a breeder, and most likely to have the dog microchipped.
- least likely to admit to putting on makeup while driving a car.
- most likely to support nuclear power.
- most likely to say that it is difficult for you to concentrate fully on the task at hand in your workplace because you are dragged down by a negative atmosphere at work.
- most likely to have a carbon monoxide detector in your home and to have an escape plan for yourself and your family in the event of fire (tied with Atlantic Canada).
- most likely to prefer e-mail as a method of communicating with your friends and least likely to be concerned that technology is taking away from face time . . . but you are also the most likely to agree that electronic communication is often used when a face-to-face meeting would be much better!

And What Is It with You People and Your Laundry?

More than other Canadians, you dislike trying to keep up with the amount of laundry in your household, and don't like dealing with your washing machine. Maybe the answer is in the fact that you do the fewest loads of laundry in a week. As well, you are most likely to strongly agree that you would enjoy doing laundry more with a nicer, newer laundry room or area—as well as new appliances. If you don't understand the logic in this paragraph, don't worry; it will all come out in the wash. Actually, while we're on this laundry thing . . . you're the most likely to admit to us that you still get your mother to do your laundry.

And Finally . . .

If stranded on a deserted island and given a choice between having food or your mobile device, you are the most likely in the country to say it's too tough to decide. Incidentally, some Canadians choose the food option because they really want to stay on the island (the weather's nice, and you hardly ever get bothered by calls from pollsters).

5 / THE QUEBECER

I f there's one thing the typical Quebecer just won't do, it's skip breakfast. Or rather, that's one of the two things Quebecers typically won't do. They're even *less* likely to skip lunch.

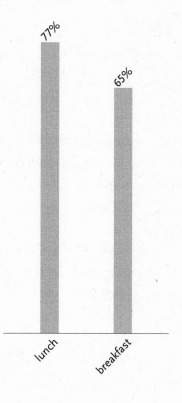

"Meals I rarely, if ever, skip."

77%

65%

lunch

breakfast

Okay, let's allow for three things a typical Quebecer won't do, because the federal constitution is still a bone of contention here, and Quebecers generally won't speak up in defence of the Senate. Given the chance, 60% would abolish it. Given a further choice between doing away with the Senate completely or reforming it into an elected body, every other region in Canada would choose reform. Quebecers still say just get rid of the whole thing.

Counting that last controversy as two decisions, we've now reached four things a typical Quebecer won't do. Heck, this calls for a top ten list, which will serve as a useful guide to local behaviour for any visitors travelling in *la belle province* this year.

Ten Things the Average Quebecer Won't Do

1) *Waste the opportunity to have some fun if they find a $100 bill by chance*

If a Quebec resident finds an extra $100 in his or her pocket, the money will go towards having fun and splurging on something, or possibly a summer vacation, but not to a charitable cause or into their savings account. In the rest of Canada, roughly half of respondents said they'd save the money or give a portion to charity. Only one-quarter of Quebecers gave this high-minded answer.

2) *Keep a ton of photographs*

Most people in Quebec own fewer than 100 printed photographs. In the rest of Canada, people have at least 200. One in five Quebecers never take pictures at all.

3) *Believe in ghosts*

Sixty-one percent say they don't believe in ghosts and spirits. Angels are another matter—a majority here do believe in angels—but even on this question Quebec is the most skeptical province, with only 57% expressing belief, compared to 71% in the rest of Canada.

4) *Take Julia Roberts to the movies*

Quebec men would rather go to a movie with their mom, or, if their mom's busy that night, they'd settle for Angelina Jolie.

5) *Defend the poor one-cent coin*

If you have affection for the penny, don't try collecting signatures of support in Quebec. Residents here are the most likely to want to get rid of it (along with the Senate).

6) Be naughty

In a Christmastime survey of all Canadians, people were asked whether Santa Claus would consider them "naughty" or "nice." Only 5% of Quebecers said "naughty." Ontarians were three times as likely (15%) to give this answer, just behind the guilt capital of Canada—Saskatchewan—where 16% confessed to naughtiness.

7) Consider themselves fat

The majority of women in the rest of Canada consider themselves to be fat. In Quebec, however, most women (60%) do not. And it's one of just two provinces where most men don't feel a bit overweight—57% describe themselves as "about right."

8) Help their partner lose weight

This one's directed at Quebec men by the women. Across Canada, 85% of women say their male partner is supportive in helping them deal with issues to do with body weight. But in Quebec, it's a completely different picture. Only one-third say their partner is supportive; two-thirds say he is not.

9) Wear pyjamas

Admittedly, the majority here is a slim one, and certainly many people in Quebec *do* wear pyjamas in bed, but overall this is the only province where it's more popular to sleep naked.

10) Snack in the morning

Probably because they're such fans of breakfast (see page 55), 91% of Quebecers don't have a morning snack.

Not Easy Being Green

When people and products get labelled "eco-friendly" or "anti-environment," it sounds as though our ecosystem is a nice simple object, something we can either love or destroy. The real story is more complicated, and so are people's attitudes. As we found out in British Columbia, people tend to be green in some ways but not in others, and opinions about the environment often seem full of contradictions.

Quebecers show great talent in producing these contradictions. Along with British Columbians, they're the most convinced that global warming is a proven fact, and generally believe that its effects have begun to happen already. Quebec homeowners lead the country in claiming to have done something to increase energy efficiency at home. At the same time, Quebecers are the least inclined to purchase a hybrid vehicle or high-efficiency home heating, and Quebec teens commonly express agreement with lackadaisical statements such as the following:

"I guess we should be mindful of the environment, but it seems like a lot of work to be environmentally friendly."

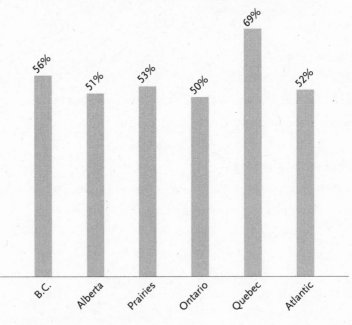

At least when it comes to water conservation, Quebec can claim the lead in switching off the garden hose over the summer, especially compared to those British Columbians.

"I stop watering the lawn during high summer."

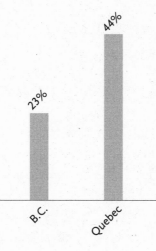

Good Arguments

Quebec residents enjoy the quality of debate among their friends and families—85% say it's either "good" or "great." The national average for this is significantly lower (73%). This province also gives the country's most generous scores to the debate in the media, the universities, and the NGOs (non-governmental organizations). It's also the harshest on politicians. Roughly a quarter of Quebecers say the quality of debate among elected politicians is terrible. People here consider debates in Canada to be too superficial and one-sided, and say that part of the problem is that Canadians are generally too reserved (84% agree with this assessment). Half of Quebec's residents say they like arguing so much that they'll get into a dispute even when they agree with the person. In this respect, they resemble many Atlantic Canadians, but fewer Manitobans.

**"I like to argue. Even if I kind of agree with someone,
I'll argue with them just for the fun of it."**

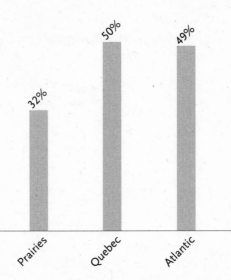

So if you wander into one those high-quality debates during a social occasion in Quebec, what are some contentious ideas you might bring up? Overall, Canadians tend to pick this as the most left-wing province in Canada; it gets chosen as such by 30% of Canadians, ahead of nearest rival British Columbia (22%). Four in ten Quebecers say they live in the most left-wing Canadian province, so that's a good general indicator of where to start a debate. In particular, though, you might choose the divisive issue of using photo radar on the highways to catch speeding vehicles, a much more controversial idea here than in the rest of Canada, with one-third of Quebecers opposed to it (surely nothing to do with fast driving habits?). Meanwhile, half the population feels there's not enough traditional traffic enforcement in their community.

If you're at a bar, you might announce that Quebecers are irresponsible beer drinkers. When that prompts an angry response, challenge a local to tell you his or her plan for getting home after consuming alcohol. Beer drinkers here are the most likely to have a relaxed attitude to such plans, and often leave it to the last minute to figure out a way home. Thirty-four percent make no plan until they're leaving the house or are already at the bar, while less than a quarter of Ontarians, British Columbians, or Atlantic Canadians are this cavalier. Incidentally, most Quebecers drank at least one beer in the past four weeks. They claim never to have been in the situation where they've already consumed alcohol and then discovered their plan for getting home has fallen through, presumably because there was no plan in the first place.

To really stir up a good argument, tell your Quebec friends that Canada should increase its military activity abroad. Quebecers consistently express the greatest opposition to foreign policies such as Canada's mission in Afghanistan. Two-thirds of the province opposed waging this war. Or downshift into an argument about intolerance towards religious people and ask why 40% of Quebecers would not vote for a political party led by a practising Muslim.

For all their skill at debating outside of the house, people in Quebec seem to have some modest trouble opening up and communicating with their romantic partner in or around the bedroom. Seventy-two percent of married Quebecers say they've wanted to talk openly with their partners about their sex lives but did not admit this desire to them. Two-thirds say, "I wish my spouse would ask me questions about myself," but they have not expressed this thought to their partners.

What Makes Quebecers Unique

If you live in Quebec, you are . . .

- *most likely to say you're doing more than most people when it comes to helping the environment.*
- *most likely to strongly agree that you spend a lot of time trying to improve your eating habits, and most likely to agree that your eating habits will help you live a long and healthy life (more poutine, please!).*

- most likely to secretly hope that your lover will spice it up for Valentine's Day.
- much more likely to purchase a product or a gift if you know that a portion of the sale will go to supporting a charitable cause.
- least likely to agree that you are prepared to pay more for an energy-efficient product.
- least likely to agree that your eating habits are probably hurting your overall health.
- (if you are 50 and older) least likely to agree that your retirement date has been delayed because of the 2008–2009 recession. So, perhaps logically, you are least likely of those 50 and older to agree that you expect to be working either full- or part-time when you are 65, and the least likely to agree that if you had enough money to retire today you would continue to work full-time.
- least likely to strongly agree that laughter is an important element in keeping sex and romance alive, and the least likely to say that a shared sense of humour is very important when it comes to sex and romance. (Seriously.)
- inclined to choose the ability to heal yourself if injured or sick (if you could possess one supernatural power).
- most likely to be really upset about an issue or passionate about something but feel you are not able to do anything about it, and therefore keep the anger bottled up inside. On the subject of taxes, for instance, you belong to the angriest bottled-up population in the country.
- the most likely in the country to choose a mobile device over food if stranded on a deserted island.
- the most prolific laundry-doers in Canada in contrast to the strange goings-on next door in Ontario with their laundry issues . . .).

AND WHAT'S THIS ABOUT YOU QUEBECERS AND CRUISE SHIPS?

Quebecers are most likely to agree that a cruise is a romantic vacation and least likely to worry about getting seasick. But wait—they are also least likely to consider a cruise for their vacation because they are least likely to agree that such a vacation would be more exciting than staying in a hotel. (Hey, what happened to the romance bit?)

AND FINALLY...

Quebecers are the most likely to have written a will. They carry documents that express their wish to donate their organs in the event of sudden death. Unlike British Columbians, they believe that organ donation should be mandatory.

People in this province rarely spend New Year's Eve quietly at home. And they think the Canadian who best represents our country is Céline Dion (more on this later).

6 / THE ATLANTIC CANADIAN

N ow, Maritimers and Newfoundlanders and Labradorians, don't go getting your sou'westers in a knot because we've put all of you in the same boat for this section of the book. We personally love the East and spend a lot of our working and vacation time there (remember the picture we wanted on the cover of this book from the red sands of Prince Edward Island?). In fact, whether it's making sure we know what people think about nuclear power in New Brunswick, business in Baddeck, hipness in Halifax, or naughtiness in Newfoundland and Labrador, we pretty much know not only what you're thinking but also what you're doing (but don't worry, Newfoundlanders, we're not under the bed). If you're wondering why the Atlantic regions get lumped together, and you skipped the bit in Chapter 3 where we made similar apologies to Prairie Canadians, well, you can flip back to that explanation, because the reasons are the same.

Meanwhile, for anyone who's not yet an Atlantic Canadian but who might consider becoming one, here's a guide to what to expect.

GOD'S COUNTRY

If you agree that touching the top of an Egyptian pyramid is no big deal compared to laying your hand on the Holy Grail, perhaps you belong among Atlantic Canadians. The east coast is the only region where the Grail wins over the other competitors on that list of things we want to touch. Four out of every five people here believe that Jesus died on the cross and was resurrected to eternal life. Half the population commit their lives to Christ. Many expect the world will end in a Battle of Armageddon between Jesus and the Antichrist.

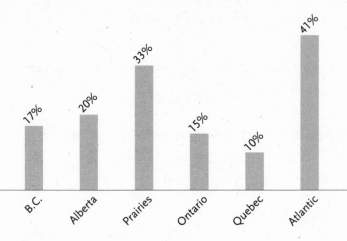

"I believe the world will end in a Battle of Armageddon."

17% B.C.
20% Alberta
33% Prairies
15% Ontario
10% Quebec
41% Atlantic

Incidentally, that figure puts Atlantic Canadians close to the average American. In the United States, 46% expect Armageddon to happen roughly as described in the Bible. (In the southern states, it's the majority view.) Four out of every ten Atlantic Canadians would not vote for a political party led by an atheist, which matches the proportion of U.S. southerners who'd refuse to vote for an atheist president.

Despite their widespread adherence to Christian beliefs, most Atlantic Canadians have never had a mystical or religious experience that gave them a sudden insight or awakening. Those moments are much more common in British Columbia. A third of the people in the eastern provinces do not attend religious services, which is a larger group than the 22% who attend once a week or more.

CANADA'S LOVE COAST

Eastern Canada has the best lovers, according to the testimony of its residents. Ninety percent of Atlantic Canadians are currently in romantic love. It is the part of the country where the fewest people get dumped at a bar. (Hearts are more commonly broken in bars on the Prairies.) And if you're a single smoker who wants to have sex on Valentine's Day, this is the place for you. Despite that wealth of romantic love, 30% of people describe themselves as "not currently in a relationship." Most say they'd date a smoker. And most single people nevertheless hope to have a wildly romantic Valentine's Day.

"I'm single, but I'm hoping next Valentine's Day will be wildly romantic."

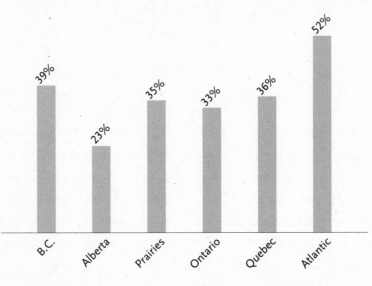

Speaking of wildly romantic, we don't quite know what to make of the next one. While this region is the least likely to say that "the woman is the boss of the household," it is the place where men want (and get) more sex than anywhere else.

Even *married* people in Atlantic Canada want more action in bed. And yes, even *middle-aged* people. As to the quality of all this loving, the numbers speak for themselves.

"I am aged 35 to 54 and my partner is a very good lover."

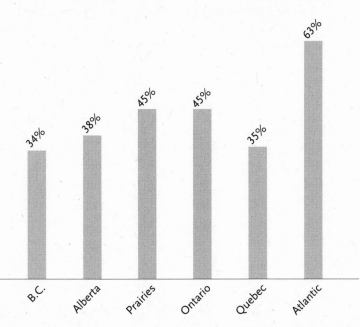

B.C. 34%
Alberta 38%
Prairies 45%
Ontario 45%
Quebec 35%
Atlantic 63%

FAMILY AND COUNTRY

Atlantic Canadians want to know their family histories. Half describe themselves as "very interested" in the topic. If a long-lost relative discovered information about them, 94% hope that person would get in touch (a quarter of Prairie residents would rather the relative left them alone). Most (70%) are curious about whether their family tree can reveal any health conditions that affect their gene pool.

Pride in Canadian culture and identity is strongest here, as is the belief that the government must strengthen culture-and-identity programs to counter the effect of increasing economic ties to the United States. Atlantic Canadians think we live in a country that's a leader in working for peace and human rights around the world, that we're a generous country, that we should take an active role in world affairs, and that we should pursue our policies independently even if it causes problems with the United States.

"I strongly believe that Canada is a generous country when it comes to giving aid to poorer countries."

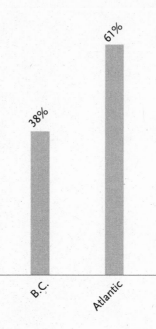

MONEY QUESTIONS

Most Atlantic Canadians don't contribute regularly to an RRSP. They live paycheque to paycheque. Sixty-eight percent agree that they should have started saving earlier. It's a common story that people from eastern provinces move west to find a better income, particularly in Alberta's oil economy, but when residents of Ontario, B.C., and Atlantic Canada were asked if they'd move to Alberta for a 25% pay increase, it was Ontario's workers who most commonly expressed willingness—29% said yes, compared to 24% from the Atlantic provinces.

This last detail may reflect on Atlantic Canadians' loyalty to their region. As in Quebec, it's more common here to say that you belong to the province than to say that your loyalties lie first and foremost with Canada. People here express affection for national symbols such as hockey, the maple leaf, Mounties, and beavers, but regional and local attachments run stronger. Among those soon to retire, Atlantic Canadians are the least likely to entertain the thought of moving to a different climate, or even to another community.

"When I retire, I want to stay right where I am."

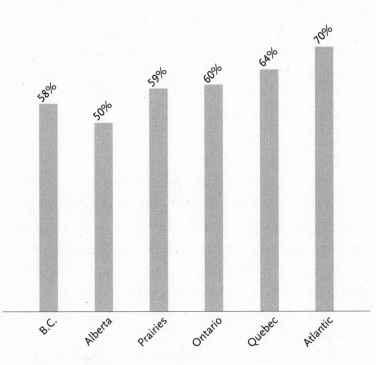

At death, an Atlantic Canadian's healthy internal organs will be transplanted to someone else who needs them. Eighty-seven percent of people want their organs to be reused, and most carry donor cards. The region is way ahead of British Columbia on this point. (Three-quarters of British Columbians are willing to have their organs trans-planted if they die, but most don't carry any documentation with them to let doctors know their wishes.)

Remember the All-Important Movie Date?

Sorry, Mom. Atlantic Canadian men would rather take Julia Roberts (25%), Angelina Jolie (21%), or even Hillary Clinton (17%) to a movie premiere. But Atlantic Canadian women can largely be counted on to turn down George Clooney in favour of their dad—four in every ten women said they'd rather go on a glitzy date with their father than with any of the offered celebrities.

What Makes Atlantic Canadians Unique

As we did with all the other regions, we now present a special tribute to what makes Easterners unique among their fellow Canadians. If you're from Atlantic Canada, you are . . .

- *most likely to agree that Canada should take serious action on climate change right now, even if it means higher deficits. You're also the most likely to agree that the Canadian government should adopt only economic stimulus measures that are environmentally sustainable.*
- *most likely to be really angry about inaction on the environment, and you are personally doing something about it. You're the most likely to say you're doing your fair share to fight climate change (and are more likely than other Canadians to agree to pay more for an energy-efficient product).*
- *most likely to agree that under President Obama the United States will do more to tackle climate change than Canada.*
- *most likely to agree that your eating habits are probably hurting your overall health and, ergo, most likely to strongly agree that your eating habits could use some improvement. The good news: You are the most likely to indicate that you have made a concerted effort to cut out junk food. Congratulations!*
- *most likely to agree that taking a cruise vacation is more exciting than staying in a hotel.*

- *least likely to strongly agree that laughter is one of the world's greatest aphrodisiacs.*
- *least likely to strongly agree that you know how to change a diaper (if you're a father expecting your first child). (A tie with Ontario fathers-to-be . . . search the Internet for "Diaper-Changing Webinar" and sign up with them.)*
- *most likely to say that you put everything in the dryer even when the label says not to. (Watch out, especially if using disposable diapers.)*
- *most likely to agree that you are able to do the type of work you best enjoy (if you're a small-business owner). (Tied with Ontario—see Business Opportunity: host diaper-changing webinars!)*
- *most likely to download a weather-update application if you're a cellphone user (no surprise here) or receive stock-market news (or here, as stocks go up and down in waves).*
- *least likely to use your mobile device for personal reasons at the grocery store, the mall, or when out with friends, but most likely to use a mobile device for organizational tasks, such as scheduling and planning time.*
- *most likely to adopt a cat from a shelter.*

AND FINALLY . . .

What is it with you people and fire? For goodness sake, almost all of you live close to, in, or around water! Yet you are the most likely to worry about having a fire in your house, the most likely to have a fire extinguisher in the house, and the most likely (tied with Ontario) to have an escape plan for you and your family in the event of fire. You're also the most likely to have a firebox for protecting important documents and valuables. Maybe it's because of all the wooden structures in Atlantic Canada?

7 / THE TRUE NORTHERNER STRONG AND FREE

N ow, if you're from Saskatchewan or Manitoba, or any province in Atlantic Canada, and you have a problem with being mushed together with your next-door neighbour in polling research, how do you think our brethren to the north feel when no one ever really reports their opinions at all? As we mentioned in the introduction to Part 1, such a small proportion of Canadians inhabit the northern territories that, when we talk to 1,000 people for a national poll and choose a group from across the country in proportion to the population in each area, we hear from only a handful of northern residents—certainly not enough to draw conclusions about what most other northerners think.

While most Canadians really don't know much about what's above the treeline (except that the real Santa Claus makes his home there), they're becoming more aware because of the impact of environmental changes to the northern coast and ocean (especially those changes causing the ice floes to thaw and the waterways to stay open)— changes that are prompting the federal government to flex its sovereignty muscles up there.

WHAT DO SOUTHERN CANADIANS THINK ABOUT THE NORTH?

Well, they're split on whether the area should be left alone by resource companies or whether miners and drillers should push ahead with exploration and development. Roughly six in ten Canadians (57%) are closer to the opinion that "the Arctic ecosystem is too fragile for the extraction of natural resources that threatens to destroy the sustainability of the ecosystem, so we should leave it relatively untouched." On the other hand, four in ten Canadians (40%) believe "that the potential of uncovering vast reserves of natural resources is too great to pass up for Canada, and that the ecosystem can be protected through careful regulation and supervision, so we should push ahead." Only 3% don't know which sentiment they more closely identify with.

Thinking about Arctic sovereignty as a matter of public policy for the government to deal with, only three in ten Canadians (28%) believe that it should be a "major priority" for the government. This places the matter well behind health care (86%), poverty (71%), the economy (69%), gas prices (67%), crime (66%), climate change (63%), and Afghanistan (46%) as major priorities for the government to tackle. In fact, a majority (51%) believe that Arctic sovereignty should be a "minor priority" for the government, while 15% believe that it is "really not a priority." Seven percent do not know how much of a priority enforcing sovereignty in the Arctic should be.

WHAT DO SOUTHERN CANADIANS THINK THE GOVERNMENT SHOULD BE DOING IN THE ARCTIC?

Thirty-nine percent believe the government should "invest serious resources in asserting Canada's sovereignty in the North, such as by building new Coast Guard icebreakers, buying new surveillance equipment, and expanding the number of troops stationed there." Thirty-two percent of Canadians think that the government should adopt a more multilateral policy and "try to work out an arrangement with the other nations to see if there is a way to accommodate everyone, even if it means Canada giving up some of its own sovereignty in the North." Twenty-six percent of Canadians would have the government adopt a more passive stance still, and agree that it should "really concentrate on other more pressing issues because we only have limited resources to deal with this, and now is not the time." Three percent don't know what the government should do going forward.

And what do these Canadians think about issues that affect their lives? Well, we have asked about that, too, and here are the results.

"Which party does the best job of understanding the needs of people like you?"

	N.W.T. (%)	Yukon (%)	Nunavut (%)
Conservatives	15	4	4
Liberals	30	17	32
NDP	29	13	31
Green Party	25	56	33
Don't know	—	10	—

	N.W.T. (%)	Yukon (%)	Nunavut (%)
I don't think the federal government has much impact on me	18	24	4
The federal government is doing too many things that should be left to businesses and individuals	27	73	63
I own a gun	45	70	50
I drink beer	76	73	50
I get migraine headaches	24	27	19

These answers don't fairly portray the people of such a vast region, a place so fragile and potentially so important in terms of energy, water, and sovereignty. The North deserves more attention, more than it's been given in school films, or on the news when visited by the governor general, the prime minister, or Pope John Paul II. We hope that we can bring you this information some day in a much more in-depth way. As soon as someone steps forward to pay for it. Anyone?

In the meantime, here's something that really occupies the thoughts of many people in the North. In the 2008 federal election, we asked northerners what issue mattered most in deciding which party's candidate they would vote for. Jobs and managing the economy fell lower on the list here than in other parts of the country. Instead, one answer towered over the rest (in some cases it was five times more popular than any other response): what motivated people was the hope of protecting the environment.

	N.W.T. (%)	Yukon (%)	Nunavut (%)
I voted mainly based on what political parties said about the environment	42	73	69

BELONGING WHERE YOU ARE

We hope these profiles give you some sense of whether you currently live in the right part of the country. If you've just realized that your true home is actually in a different province or region, we wish you the best of luck with your upcoming move. But before you pack those bags, it's worth considering what else might affect the minds of Canadians around you. After all, not *every* Manitoban believes in ghosts, not *every* British Columbian thinks it's okay to water the lawn all summer, and not *every* Atlantic Canadian is a patriotic Christian with a raging libido. A person could commit all kinds of social faux pas by making assumptions based on just one set of data.

Besides that, can't Canadians claim a greater shared sense of nation-hood, way beyond the little distinctions between east and west? Isn't there anything that collectively defines us? (Cue the national anthem, please.)

Funny you should ask . . .

PART TWO / WHO ARE WE, EH?

8 / THE NATION-DEFINING SURVEY

In conjunction with the Dominion Institute and the Department of Citizenship and Immigration, we conducted the Nation-Defining Survey in order to discover the people, places, events, accomplishments, and symbols that Canadians believe represent their country. Here are the most popular answers in each category.

- *Person:* Pierre Trudeau
- *Place:* Niagara Falls
- *Event:* Canada Day
- *Accomplishment:* Canadarm
- *Symbol:* Maple leaf

The questionnaire went on to ask Canadians to give top ten rankings in each category. We did some math, and came up with the national rankings. Here they are.

People

Canadians say Pierre Trudeau is the person who most defines what it is to be Canadian, followed by Wayne Gretzky and Terry Fox. Céline Dion is fourth, while Sir John A. Macdonald rounds out the top five. The next five down the list are David Suzuki, Tommy Douglas, Stephen Harper, Lester Pearson, and Maurice Richard.

Pierre Trudeau led the pack in every province or region of Canada except for Alberta (Wayne Gretzky) and Quebec (Céline Dion). Interestingly, in British Columbia, activist Rick Hansen placed in the top ten (at number seven). Meanwhile, in Saskatchewan and Manitoba,

Tommy Douglas made it into third place and Queen Elizabeth II was in ninth place.

Places

Niagara Falls is apparently the location that most clearly defines Canada, while the Rocky Mountains place second. Parliament Hill, Ottawa, and Toronto's CN Tower make up the rest of the top five. The next four are all cities: Quebec City, Toronto, Montreal, and Vancouver.

In western Canada, the Rocky Mountains easily win first place, while eastern Canadians choose either Niagara Falls (the choice of Ontarians) or Parliament Hill (the choice of Quebecers and Atlantic Canadians). Other appearances on the list include Fort Garry (seventh place in Saskatchewan and Manitoba), Charlottetown (sixth place in Atlantic Canada), and Fort Louisbourg (eighth place in Atlantic Canada).

Events

Overall, Canada Day is the most defining event in Canada, followed by Confederation and the two world wars. The Calgary Stampede and the Battle of Vimy Ridge are next in the rankings, followed by the Battle at the Plains of Abraham, the Grey Cup, the Olympics, Expo 67, and the Quebec Winter Carnival.

Canada Day is the first choice across all provinces and regions, without any disagreement. After first place, however, regions appear to be biased towards events that happen in their own backyard. Examples of this include the Calgary Stampede (second place in Alberta) and the Battle at the Plains of Abraham (second place in Quebec).

Accomplishments

Canadians believe that the *Canadarm* is the most defining accomplishment in Canadian history, with Canada's peacekeeping forces second on the list. Universal health care, the discovery of insulin, and the invention of the telephone round out the top five. The next five are: diversity, the Canadian Constitution, the Canadian National Railway, freedom, and the Avro Arrow project.

But here again, the supposed "Canadian favourite" depends on support from the big populations of Quebec and Ontario—the only provinces to put the Canadarm in pole position. Other regions chose universal health care (British Columbia, Saskatchewan, and Manitoba) and peacekeeping (Alberta and Atlantic Canada). Canadians living in Alberta express particular pride in Canada's oil industry (ninth place), while our country's bilingualism strikes a chord in the Prairies (tenth place) and Atlantic Canada (ninth place).

Symbols

The first-place symbol of Canada as chosen by the Canadian population coast to coast is the maple leaf. Following are hockey, the Canadian flag, the beaver, and the RCMP. Rounding out the top ten are the Stanley Cup, wilderness, the Loonie, maple syrup, and moose or caribou.

While the maple leaf wins in every province, the next four spots are shuffled considerably from province to province. Some more offbeat images appear farther down the regional rankings, including the Château Frontenac (sixth place in Quebec), the *Bluenose* (sixth place in Atlantic Canada), the Canada Goose, and wheat (ninth and tenth place respectively in Saskatchewan and Manitoba).

So much for national identity. But all of this raises a question you should be asking yourself (see, we not only tell you what you're thinking, we also tell you what you should ask): Why is there a donut on this book's cover when it doesn't rank among the top five symbols? Great question! Because Canadians eat more donuts per capita than any other country on earth! That's why your two slightly plump pollsters think it should be out national dish.

WHAT CANADIANS KNOW ABOUT CANADA'S PAST

As pollsters whose work frequently finds its way onto the front pages of newspapers all over the country, we try our best to be fair—fair to the issues, fair to the people who answer our questions, and fair to the people who read our results. But there's one thing we do that, although it's not exactly *unfair*, it tends not to show Canadians in their best light. A couple of times a year, we test citizens' knowledge of basic facts about the country, its history, its political system, and so on. Generally speaking, these tests reveal how startlingly ignorant most of us are! A word of comfort, then: We suspect that many people, when suddenly put on the spot with a pop quiz about Canadian culture, forget facts or make errors that, on another day, in a more relaxed situation, they might remember—or at least guess at more accurately.

WHAT WE CANADIANS DON'T KNOW

- *We don't know in which war the Battle of Vimy Ridge took place.* (By the way, it was the First World War. Roughly one-third of Canadians can answer this correctly.)
- *We don't know who Canada fought in the First World War.* Fewer than one in five Canadians can name Austria-Hungary or Turkey as well as Germany when listing our opponents in 1914.
- *We don't know why Remembrance Day is on November 11.* Slightly more than one-third (37%) correctly tell pollsters that it marks the last day of the First World War.
- *We can't name a war in which the United States invaded Canada.* Only 30% can reel off the names "The War of Independence" or "The War of 1812" when quizzed.
- *We don't know what happened on D-Day.* A minority of Canadians can tell pollsters immediately that this was the day when Allied forces landed in Normandy.

- *We don't know which prime minister won a Nobel Peace Prize for resolving the Suez Crisis.* As significant as Lester Pearson's achievement was at the time, today only one out of ten Canadians can link his name to this event.
- *We have no idea what you need in order to vote.* Ninety-six percent, or to put it more literally, 964 people out of the 1,000 we asked, could not name all three requirements for taking part in our democracy's major event, the federal election. Most of us know you have to be a citizen, and about half of us realize that it's essential to have reached your eighteenth birthday, but almost everyone forgot that you have to be registered to vote. Instead of this last requirement, people came up with all kinds of possible ones for voting, none of which hit the mark. Many people believe you can't be in prison; others think you just need to reside in this country; some reckon that the government checks that voters have "a sound mind" (this one might be a good idea, but would be complicated to enforce); and an optimistic few even believe people are required to have "knowledge of the issues"! Now that really is crazy.
- *We don't know what the government expects of its citizens.* The official line from Citizenship and Immigration Canada is that citizens have a particular list of responsibilities: we're supposed to vote in elections, obey the law, respect each other's rights, help our fellow citizens, care for Canada's heritage, eliminate discrimination,* and protect the environment. Unfortunately, only 3% of Canadians seem to have read this list or to be able to guess at it. The people we asked usually fumbled about with other possible responsibilities, such as paying taxes and being loyal to Canada or the Queen, finding a job, serving or defending the country,

---

*Editor's Note: This presumably refers to "unfair discrimination" rather than the general faculty of discriminating, which is the ability to distinguish and choose between alternatives.

taking care of kids, and being generally "responsible." Most of these might fall under the category of obeying the law, of course. By the way, the least-known official citizen duty is the one about caring for heritage. Out of the 1,000 people we consulted, only six individuals mentioned this concept. Four of them had gone to university, and may actually have been law professors.

- *We don't know which provinces joined together in Confederation.* Eighty-four percent of Canadians cannot name the original four as Ontario, Quebec, New Brunswick, and Nova Scotia. People tend to replace either or both of the last two with Manitoba, Prince Edward Island, Saskatchewan, or Alberta. Even more commonly, people just admit they don't know (one-fifth of those we contacted decided it was best not to even try answering this question).

- *We don't know what the Charter of Rights and Freedoms is.* It seems Canadians' love of Pierre Trudeau can survive without needing to know much about his signature achievement. When asked to name the part of the Constitution that legally protects basic rights and freedoms, only one in three people point to the Charter (and many of these people just call it the "Charter of Rights," which, if we were being really picky, falls short of its full title). About one in ten Canadians hazard a guess that it's the Human Rights Act, but it's much more common just to plead, "Don't know." Only a tiny fraction of the population can name four of the "rights and freedoms" protected.

- *We can't count the provinces and territories correctly.* Only one in three Canadians can tell you that the country comprises ten provinces and three territories. All manner of combinations are suggested by the other two-thirds of people.

- *We're unsure about the Queen's job.* Most Canadians think that either the prime minister or the governor general is this country's head of state. Fewer than one in ten believe, as is correct, that the Queen is officially in charge of the country.

- *We know the Hudson's Bay Company traded furs.* Two-thirds of Canadians correctly identify "fur" or "beaver" as the main item historically traded and controlled by the Hudson's Bay Company. Only one in twenty people suggested the answer was "Zellers" or "running a department store." Fur trading has declined in the Canadian psyche, however. Ten years ago, three-quarters gave the correct answer to this question.

- *We've heard of "Confederation."* By a statistical knife-edge, Canada can claim that a majority of its citizens know the word for the country's formation out of individual provinces. Five and a half out of ten Canadians can give the name "Confederation." Most people who did not attend university, and most people earning under $30,000 a year, cannot give this answer.

- *We know which province has the most bilingual Canadians.* Actually, this one is really a tie, because in our test 52% of people got it right and 48% got it wrong, which falls within that pesky "margin of error," so the next time we do the same test we might find those numbers get flipped. In any case, the province with the most bilingual Canadians is Quebec. An outnumbered but very large group of people think it's Ontario or New Brunswick.

- *We know the name of our national anthem.* "O Canada"—practically everyone knows this one. And most of us can even sing the first line.

- *We know which oceans border the country.* Only a fraction of the population—perhaps just 750,000 adults in total—believes that, Canada borders the Antarctic Ocean. Which is quite a lot of people, when you think about it.

- *We can name four of the Great Lakes.* Most Canadians who earn more than $30,000 per year or who attended a college or university can name four of the five biggest ponds in North America.

- *We know Prince Edward Island is (geographically) the smallest province.* Only a few Canadians, roughly one in twenty, believe that Newfoundland is smaller than Prince Edward Island.
- *We're aware of the United States.* Nine out of ten Canadians can name the United States as our largest trading partner.
- *We remember the prime minister's name.* The name of the current prime minister eludes only one out of every five Canadians. Roughly a quarter of the people who did not stay in the education system after high school can't name the prime minister. That's about the same as the proportion of Canadians who can't name the political party governing their province or territory.

OKAY, NOW FOR SOME REALLY TRICKY ONES

How is the prime minister elected?

Canadians are split on how the prime minister of Canada is elected. While one-half (51%) believe that he or she is directly elected, the other half (49%) do not.

Quebecers (70%) are most likely to believe that prime ministers are directly elected by the people of Canada, making that province the only region where a majority believes this. A minority of those in British Columbia (49%), Ontario (47%), Saskatchewan and Manitoba (44%), Alberta (42%), and Atlantic Canada (35%) think that prime ministers are directly elected.

In contrast, a majority of Atlantic Canadians (65%) do not believe that prime ministers are elected in this manner, and the same can be said about those living in Alberta (58%), Saskatchewan and Manitoba (56%), Ontario (53%), and British Columbia (51%). Only three in ten Quebecers (30%) believe this.

The right answer is that the Canadian prime minister is not directly elected to office. Instead, our constitution works with the convention that whoever leads the political party with the most elected members gets asked to take the job.

Who is Canada's head of state?

Much confusion exists regarding who is Canada's head of state. Forty-two percent believe that it's the prime minister. Thirty-three percent think this title belongs to the governor general. Only 24% of Canadians knows that Canada's head of state is the Queen.

How is Canada's government best described?

Six in ten Canadians (59%) were able to identify Canada correctly as a "constitutional monarchy." Four in ten gave an incorrect response, believing that it was best described as a "cooperative assembly" (25%) or a "representative republic" (17%).

Ontarians (63%) and residents of Saskatchewan and Manitoba (63%) are most likely to know that Canada is a constitutional monarchy, while Albertans (61%), Atlantic Canadians (60%), and Quebecers (57%) are only slightly less likely to know this. However, British Columbians are most likely to think that we live in a cooperative assembly (28%) or a representative republic (24%).

Can the governor general refuse the prime minister?

Nine in ten Canadians (90%) believe that the governor general has the power to refuse the prime minister's request for an election. Just 10% do not.

Albertans (97%) are the most likely to know this, followed by Canadians living in Atlantic Canada (96%), Saskatchewan and Manitoba (92%), Ontario (89%), British Columbia (88%), and Quebec (86%). What's the right answer? Actually, constitutional lawyers dispute this one. But under certain circumstances, the governor general can refuse.

Thoughts on What a Citizen Actually Is

Dual Citizenship

Four in ten Canadians are against the current policy regarding dual citizenship, and believe that Canadians should not be allowed to simultaneously hold citizenship in more than one country.

Seventy-five percent of Canadians aged 18 to 34 believe that Canadians should be able to hold dual citizenship. However, the propensity to agree with this concept changes with age. Indeed, only about 50% of Canadians 55 and older agree that we should be allowed to hold dual citizenship.

Owning a Canadian flag

Demonstrating their patriotism, six in ten Canadians maintain that someone in their household owns a Canadian flag. Among those who do have a flag, one-half say that they fly it in their yard or display it in a window.

Older Canadians are more likely to report that someone in their household owns a Canadian flag, with two-thirds of them indicating so. In comparison, just half of the younger Canadians we spoke to indicate that someone in their household owns a flag.

Seven in ten Albertans say that someone in their household owns a Canadian flag, which is close to the results from Ontario and Atlantic Canada (each at 68%). Just a quarter of households in Quebec report that they own a Canadian flag.

Ontarians are the most likely to display their flags, with six in ten indicating that they do so. Fifty-three percent of Atlantic Canadians also display them. Just one-quarter of Quebecers whose household owns a Canadian flag report that that it is on display in the yard or in a window.

Older Canadians are more likely than younger ones to display their Canadian flag, with six in ten of those aged 55 and older indicating that their household's flag is on display, while only four in ten Canadians aged 18 to 34 indicate the same.

So How Are We Doing, Patriotically Speaking?

After a decade of publicly released polls, educational programs, and national events and discussions on citizenship, electoral efficacy, and immigration aimed at youth, things seem to be getting, well, worse. This is despite the great work of the Dominion Institute of Canada, a treasured not-for-profit institution. Ten years after our first survey, we asked Canadians aged 18 to 24 the same questions. And the impact of all the efforts by patriots and nationalists? Hmm . . . you be the judge.

- In British Columbia, only 15% (down from 23% a decade ago) passed the quiz.
- Alberta still performed ahead of the national average with 22% (but down from 27%).
- In Saskatchewan and Manitoba, 29% passed the quiz (up from the 16% who passed it ten years ago, giving them the largest increase in knowledge in the decade among any region in the country).
- In Ontario, 21% passed the quiz (down from 23%).
- In Quebec, only 9% passed the quiz (down from 12%).
- In Atlantic Canada, 13% passed the quiz (down from 18%).
- On the gender split: 24% of men passed (no change) and 12% of women passed (down from 14%).

Subjects that actually showed improvement
- 32% (up from 17%) know that Chinese Canadians were forced to pay a head tax to immigrate to Canada.
- 37% (up from 31%) know that the Battle of Vimy Ridge was fought in the First World War.

- 37% (up from 33%) know that November 11 marked the final day of World War I.
- 29% (up from 26%) can identify either the War of 1812, the Revolutionary War, or the War of Independence as a war in which Canada was invaded by the United States.
- 35% (up from 32%) identify the Acadians as the French-speaking early settlers of what is now New Brunswick and Nova Scotia who were expelled by the British.
- 41% (up 3from 8%) identify Halifax as the Canadian city that was severely damaged by a massive explosion in 1917.

Responses that showed we're getting more clueless
- 46% (down from 54%) know that John A. Macdonald was the first Canadian prime minister.
- 26% (down from 36%) know that 1867 was the year of Confederation.
- 56% (down from 67%) know that Wilfrid Laurier was Canada's first francophone prime minister.
- 52% (down from 65%) name Louis-Joseph Papineau as the leader of a nineteenth-century rebellion in Quebec.
- 38% (down from 51%) know that Newfoundland was the last province to join Confederation.
- 27% (down from 40%) know that Louis Riel was hanged by the federal government in 1885.
- 22% (down massively from 60%) know that Free Trade was the economic issue that dominated the elections of 1891, 1911, and 1988.

THE (ALMOST FOR REAL) CITIZENSHIP TEST FOR CANADIANS

This country might be proud of Pierre Trudeau, but he probably wouldn't be too proud of the country's results in the mock citizenship test we conducted. People who completed a university degree usually squeaked by with a passing grade, but most people who didn't—

and that means most Canadians overall—failed the sort of test that immigrants are expected to pass in order to attain citizenship. Sure, plenty more people would have passed if they'd had to study the same materials that immigrants must read and prepare properly for the citizenship exam rather than giving shoot-from-the-hip answers to our online poll. What our mock test shows, however, is that, from day to day, Canadians don't find it necessary to know very much about the country's history, geography, and politics in order to live their lives and feel proud of their nation.

You, however, have just read most of the answers, so you could probably pass with flying colours. If you've got a couple of minutes to spare for your country right now, place that foam maple leaf hat on your head and tackle the citizenship test that stumped most Canadians.

MOCK CITIZENSHIP TEST

1. Name three requirements that a person must meet in order to vote in a federal election.
2. Name three responsibilities that Canadian citizens hold.
3. What was the main trade controlled by the Hudson's Bay Company?
4. When the first provinces joined to form Canada, what was that event called?
5. Which four provinces joined together in Confederation?
6. What is the part of the constitution that legally protects the basic rights and freedoms of all Canadians?
7. Name four different rights and/or freedoms protected by the Canadian Charter of Rights and Freedoms.
8. Which province has the most bilingual Canadians?
9. Which song is Canada's national anthem?
10. What are the the first two lines of the national anthem?
11. What three oceans border Canada?

12. How many provinces and territories are there in Canada?
13. Name four of the five Great Lakes.
14. Which province in Canada is the smallest in land size?
15. Which country is Canada's largest trading partner?
16. Who is Canada's head of state?
17. What are the three levels of government in Canada?
18. Name all four of the federal political parties presently represented in the House of Commons.
19. What is the name of the prime minister of Canada?
20. In the federal parliament, what is a law called before it is passed?
21. Which political party is in power in your province or territory?

Now, find out if you'd get to stay in this country or get the boot! (If you don't pass, then perhaps you are secretly an American—we'll check out that possibility in the next section.)

ANSWERS TO THE MOCK CITIZENSHIP TEST

1. You must be a Canadian citizen, you must be 18 years old, and you must be a registered or "enumerated" voter.
2. The responsibility to vote in elections, obey Canadian law, respect others' rights, help others, care for Canada's heritage, eliminate discrimination, and protect the environment.
3. Fur or beaver.
4. Confederation.
5. Ontario, Quebec, New Brunswick, Nova Scotia.
6. The Charter of Rights and Freedoms.
7. Freedom of conscience/religion;
   freedom of belief/opinion/expression/the press/the media;
   the right to peaceful assembly, association;
   the right to vote;
   the right to mobility, life/liberty/security of the person;

freedom from unreasonable search or seizure, freedom from
   arbitrary detention or imprisonment;

the right to be informed of reasons for arrest, to retain counsel,
   to habeas corpus;

the right to a speedy trial, a trial by jury;

freedom from double jeopardy;

the right not to be subjected to cruel and unusual punishment;

the right to equality;

the right to use official languages;

legal rights;

democratic rights; and

the right to racial equality.

8. Quebec.

9. "O Canada."

10. O Canada! / Our home and native land.

11. Atlantic, Arctic, Pacific.

12. Ten provinces and three territories.

13. Erie, Huron, Ontario, Superior, Michigan.

14. Prince Edward Island.

15. The United States of America.

16. Queen Elizabeth II.

17. Federal, provincial, municipal.

18. Conservative, Liberal, New Democratic, Bloc Québécois.

19. You'll have to check the news for this one.

20. A bill.

21. See 19.

9 / THE SOUTHERN REGION OVER THE BORDER

I t's tough being in the shadow of a superpower. It produces a kind
of schizophrenia in which we like to glide below the radar of the
United States and do our own thing, yet hope we'll get noticed like
some deserving fan. And when we do get noticed, it's a little like Sally
Field's Oscar acceptance speech in 1985, in which she exclaimed, "You
like me, right now, you like me!"

So What's the Difference?
People always ask us, "So, how are we different from Americans?"
thinking that we'll tell them our attitudes and outlooks are a yawn-
ing gulf apart. But they're not. Just like the differences among the
regions of our country, the differences we see with the United States
are not verwhelmingly profound. Said another way, the differences
are matters of degree. It's like the word "sorry"—an American will
say that he's "*saw-ree*," while a Canadian will say that he's "*sore-ee*."
We're both apologizing, but we say it just a little differently. In fact, an
English-speaker from another place probably wouldn't hear the difference. For the most part, that's how much the opinions and attitudes of
Americans and Canadians differ on the big questions. Very little.

Our two nations have some solid institutional differences: the
American political system is made up predominantly of two parties,
one right-wing and one left-wing. They have a right to guns and we
don't; they have a different health care system, which, despite the
efforts of President Obama, is and will likely remain overwhelmingly
private and profit-based while a few more public services nudge in.

Ours, on the other hand, will remain overwhelmingly public and government-funded, while more private, for-profit services nudge *their* way in. We have a very tightly regulated banking and financial system and they, er, well, we're not sure any more. Their enshrined ideals are *Life, Liberty, and the Pursuit of Happiness* and ours are the principles of *Peace, Order, and Good Government.* They have a political checks-and-balances system among the president, the congress, and the Supreme Court, and we have, well, the auditor general and the parliamentary budget officer and the governor general, a representative of the Queen (who is our head of state). We have loonies and toonies and they have greenbacks.

SOCIAL ATTITUDES

Now, some pollsters and supposedly learned folk have made a bit of a name for themselves when it comes to comparing the underlying social attitudes held by people in Canada and the United States. According to their theories, one of two things is happening. The first is that Canada is slowly but surely drifting into a closer relationship with the United States—in fact, some writers have even predicted that Canada's ultimate destiny is nothing less than complete absorption into the American republic. The other argument is that Canadians and Americans are actually becoming increasingly different and are drifting apart, from a values perspective.

Sorry, but we just don't buy either definitive take on the supposed worlds of difference. It might make for entertaining after-dinner speeches and a book or two, but it does not hold up under the scrutiny of long-tracked data. We've been polling and comparing attitudes of Americans and Canadians for a long time, and let us share with you what we think is going on: Many Americans are becoming more like us. Yup, and this is not based on a post–George W. Bush/collapse of capitalism flurry of polls that, again, might skew things one way or the other immediately following a major assault on fundamental thinking of American society.

Now, we can't use this limited space to put a book within a book on our Northern Cross-Border Convergence: From American to Americanuck theory, but here's a smattering of what we've witnessed.

"The government has a responsibility to take care of the poor."

	Canada (%)	U.S. (%)
1992	83	69
1997	81	61
2005	87	78

"The government has a responsibility to take care of the elderly."

	Canada (%)	U.S. (%)
1992	88	75
1997	87	78
2005	93	88

"People from different racial and cultural backgrounds would be better off if they became more like the majority."

	Canada (%)	U.S. (%)
1992	50	39
1997	44	37
2005	53	41

In sum, what these data show is that majorities in both Canada and the United States feel that we have a responsibility, through our governments, to take care of the poor and the elderly. While these numbers have remained pretty consistent in Canada over the tracking period, the public support has grown stronger—more Canadian, we might say—in the United States.

How Different Are We?

On the question of racial and cultural convergence, *Canadians* are the ones who have less tolerance for difference than Americans. Wait a tick. Isn't it supposed to be exactly the opposite? Let's try a little quiz. Here are some questions from the December 2008 wave of Ipsos' 23-country poll called "Global @dvisor." The results presented are for Canada and the United States. Which numbers go with which country?

Opinion	Country A (%)	Country B (%)
I have a positive opinion of the beer industry.	39	33
I have a positive opinion of the fast food industry.	24	39
I have a positive opinion of the banking industry.	37	24
Expanding trade is a good thing.	88	79
Overall, globalization is a good thing for the world.	68	57
Overall, globalization is a good thing for my country.	68	63
We should restrict investment by foreign companies in my country, even if it means fewer jobs will be created.	33	44

Canada is "Country A." Yup, go figure. Canadians like the beer industry and Americans like the fast food industry. Canadians like their banks and are more comfortable with the private sector, foreign investment, globalization, and freer trade than Americans. The bottom line here is that Canadians may need to check their prejudices at the door when they talk about America. As you can see from the data, the differences on many questions are less profound than we might think, and might work in a different direction than we assume.

One issue on which there is a consistent difference between American and Canadian is the role of government in society. Americans are typically about 10 points lower than Canadians on nearly every question we ask. But the point is that in many instances we're talking about differences between two majorities. To us, that's like the difference in how we say "sorry."

Turning to the similarities between Canada and the United States, there are many examples that we can point to. Here are just a few:

Opinion	Canada (%)	U.S. (%)
Large companies have too much influence on the decisions of my government.	83	84
The government of my country should be more aggressive in regulating the activities of national and multinational corporations.	84	74
Large companies are more powerful than governments.	82	73
Foreign companies have too much control and influence over the economy in my country.	71	71
CEOs of large companies can generally be trusted to tell the truth when they make statements about their company or their industry.	18	17
Government regulation of big businesses and corporations is necessary to protect the public.	73	67

Opinion	Canada (%)	U.S. (%)
Companies should pay more attention to the environment.	92	84
Companies should do more to contribute to society.	82	78

And, finally, one of our very favourite questions is about generational progress. In other words, will the next generation fare better than the current one? For us, this is the ultimate question about social progress and optimism. Do you think your kids will do better than you? Here's what we ask: "When children in your country grow up, do you think they will be better off or worse off than people are right now?"

When we asked this question in December 2008, 40% told us "better" and 60% said "worse" in both the United States and Canada. So, even with 9/11, the war on terror, the great economic disruption, and George Bush, Jr., both Canadians and Americans have ended up in exactly the same place when it comes to optimism. Go figure.

Now, let's turn for a moment to politics, or what we like to call "sports for the un-coordinated," or "show business for ugly people." After the election of Barack Obama as president of the United States, three-quarters (76%) of Canadians thought his victory was a good thing—up a full 50 points compared with data collected on the eve of President Bush's second inauguration in 2004, when only 26% thought his re-election was a good idea. Just 3% said Obama's election was a bad thing, whereas 8% saw both good and bad in the new president's arrival, 6% saw it as "neither," and 7% said they didn't know. To underscore how much Canadians like Barack Obama, we asked a question during the 2008 federal election that included Obama as a potential prime minister for Canada. According to the answers, Obama would have easily formed a majority government!

Going back to President Bush, who has been given a tough ride over both his foreign and domestic policies, three-quarters (72%) of

Canadians disagree (44% strongly and 28% somewhat) that "the critics of George Bush have been too harsh and people will think much better of his presidency in the future." Conversely, three in ten (28%) agree (5% strongly and 22% somewhat) that people will come around to poor "Dubya" in the long run.

Residents of Quebec (81%) and British Columbia (80%) are most likely to disagree with that sentiment, followed by those living in Atlantic Canada (72%), Ontario (67%), Alberta (66%), and Saskatchewan and Manitoba (64%).

As for President Barack Obama, at the outset of his presidency, most Canadians (86%) agreed that he gave them great hope for the future of America and the world. Atlantic Canadians (93%) and Quebecers (92%) were the most hopeful; Prairie Canadians (67%) were the least smitten with optimism.

On the issues, however, Canadians didn't express so much hope.

The issue	Things will get better with Obama as president	Things will stay the same	Expect the worst
Border security	31	63	5
Cross-border transit of people, goods, and services	34	60	7
Dealing with trade disputes	38	52	10
Recognizing Canada's ownership of the Arctic	27	63	10
The regulation of financial markets	43	52	5
Forest and industry complaints by U.S. counterparts	25	62	13
The Canadian auto-manufacturing industry	25	60	15

Despite being critical of many of the policies that the American government has undertaken in the past while, six in ten Canadians "like and admire Americans, that is, citizens of the United States"— results that are unchanged from those of our 2005 poll.

Some of you might have just discovered that you fit more easily with the trend of U.S. public opinion than with that of any of the regions of Canada. But don't pack your bags and head to the U.S. immigration office yet! You might still find that you're among your people. And in fact, if you really want to predict what another Canadian probably thinks, you'll need to bear in mind a few more of the great forces shaping his or her life. Some of the biggest differences between human beings depend on whether they grew up male or female, so after you've collected your citizenship papers, be sure to proceed quickly to the next chapter.

10 / THE MAN AND THE WOMAN

M en and women have written insightful things about each other for centuries, so we ought to understand the two sexes pretty well by now. We can appreciate the point the late Princess Diana made in 1984 after the birth of her second son; she said that if men had to give birth, they would have only one baby and never repeat the experience. Today, we can look into the eyes of any woman who does not have a man in her life and see that she really is like a fish without a bicycle. The humorous comparison of man-less women to bicycle-less fish (attributed by Gloria Steinem to Irina Dunn) makes sense to roughly half the women we asked, although fewer men seemed to appreciate the joke.

And thanks to the Romantic poet Lord Byron, how could anybody deny that "Man's love is of man's life a thing apart / 'Tis a woman's whole existence"? Okay, plenty of people deny that. Three out of ten Canadians disagree with Byron's idea, but that leaves seven out of ten who agree, quite a solid body of support considering that he came to the conclusion two centuries ago.

The sad fact is that all the combined genius of our poets, writers, and princesses has not been enough to mend the divide between men and women and allow them to make sense of each other. Luckily, our pollsters here at Ipsos have leaped bravely into that divide so that, with the tact and delicacy of marriage guidance counsellors, they could finally sort out exactly where Canadian males stand in relation to Canadian females. And now we can tell you what we found.

THE CANADIAN WOMAN . . .

She believes in ghosts and wants to watch the Oscars but . . . put a bunch of people on the couch, switch on the television, and watch her *not* end up with the remote control. She's glad that Canada does not have the death penalty, and wishes we would stop killing seals, too. Yes, the rumours are true—she'd rather have chocolate. It is, she believes, completely acceptable to ask barbeque guests to bring their own meat. She does not feel that, in general, preschool children suffer if both parents take jobs instead of staying at home. She figures $750,000 should be enough for a comfortable retirement, and when she retires she'd love to have a professional snow-shovelling and lawn-mowing service available where she lives. If her partner ignored Valentine's Day, she'd feel a little bit sad.

. . . THE CANADIAN MAN

He is pretty much the opposite.

PROBABLY MAYBE

Okay, one more caveat before we get carried away here. Statistics from opinion polls suggest the way a person *probably* thinks, but that word "probably" can be a long, long distance from "certainly." If all you know about a person is that she is a woman—you don't even know where she lives except that it's somewhere between Tofino and Peggys Cove—then you can guess that she might believe in ghosts. Slightly less than half of the time, though, you'd be wrong.

"I am a Canadian woman and I believe in ghosts."

53% 46%

yes no

If you have *two* Canadians, a man and a woman, and just one of them believes in ghosts . . . well, you can guess it'll be the woman. And, six times out of ten, you'll be right. Probably.

"I am a Canadian and I believe in ghosts."

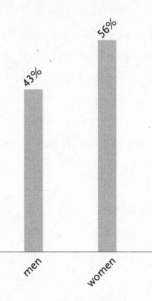

HOW TO GET ALONG

Forget the glossy magazines with their tips on understanding your man and the pop-psychology experts on television with their best-selling theories. Here's how the battle of the sexes can be peacefully resolved, according to the latest information from opinion polls.

STEP ONE: EARLY IMPRESSIONS

If a Canadian woman sits in the passenger seat of a car while on a romantic excursion with a man—let's say it's their second date—she probably has lip balm with her and a pack of gum, and doesn't want to listen to heavy metal. If she doesn't have lip balm or gum, she probably wants some, so the man could win brownie points by keeping these items in the glove compartment.

If the woman is hoping the man will park the car so the two of them can kiss, she's probably keeping her eye open for some sort of beach, if one is available in that part of the country.

What are women's favourite places to park for a romantic roadside moment?

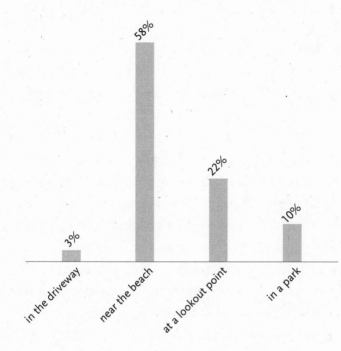

If there's no beach, the man could try to inspire romantic feelings in the woman by giving her flowers, but a word of advice for anyone following this well-travelled route: remember that a majority of women prefer to receive flowering plants that can live in the garden, rather than cut flowers. The important point for the man here is not to get carried away with the gardening idea, because the goal of a romantic gift is not to provide serious horticultural assistance. In fact only 2% of Canadian women would choose gardening tools as their perennial favourite Valentine's Day treat.

The eyes have it. Women judge men by their smile and eyes, and don't consider eyeglasses sexy. More women will get their hair coloured this year than will visit an optometrist. Eighty percent of Canadian women own and sometimes wear eyeglasses.

STEP TWO: "GETTING" THE DREAM

Gifts can help a man please a woman in the short term, but long-term relationships call for more profound demonstrations of understanding. A man ought to be aware of a woman's ambitions, even—or perhaps *most of all*—when they aren't yet being fulfilled. For instance, many women want to switch careers and work in the medical profession, which is an option that hardly ever occurs to men who aren't already doctors or med students. Accountancy and banking spark the enthusiasm of many more women, so it might be a bad plan for a man to mock those professions as being dull or unpleasant, as this risks belittling how a woman imagines her future. But most of all, women aspire to work for the government or in the entertainment business, two very different directions! A smart man will figure out the direction a particular woman's dreams point to—the realm of public service with benefits, or the realm of performance and glamour.

STEP THREE: GOOD HABITS

After initially impressing a woman with his at-the-ready supply of lip balm and his prescient understanding of her career dreams, every Canadian man must eventually reveal his personal habits.

According to opinion poll data, the men most likely to impress are non-smokers who look at one or two newspapers a day and manage to be aware of local issues, while offering "good home cooking" or "simple fare—whatever is in the fridge or in the cupboards," as well as moderately "warm" behaviour in bed rather than raging sexual desire or cold indifference. (This preference is expressed by three-quarters of Canadian women.) Perhaps most importantly, women want men to do whatever is needed around the house, with one in five women going as far as recommending that a man be "neat and tidy, spic and span" in order to impress them. The two sexes approach tidying a bit differently, however. We gave people a list and asked them to imagine that everything on the list had become cluttered or disorganized and needed attention. We asked which area they would tackle first. Here's the list:

- closets
- bills and finances
- personal photos
- kitchen cupboards
- don't know

Men headed straight for the bills and finances. Most women chose one of the other options.

As for the other tasks, men and women both claim to thoroughly clean their home on a daily or weekly basis. Only 15% of Canadians say they thoroughly clean the house every other week or less. Men are a bit more likely to get the most satisfaction from cleaning the living room or family room; more women say the kitchen is the most satisfying place to clean. Men and women agree that the bathroom, basement, and attic are their least favourite. Three-quarters agree that cleaning is better than ironing. The other quarter

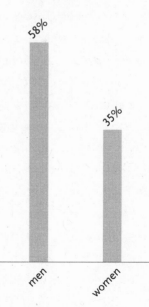

"I'd go for the bills and finances first."

58%

35%

men

women

say they'd rather iron or, even better, avoid both activities. Based on this statistic, either partner would gain more brownie points by ironing the other's clothes than by cleaning a room.

STEP FOUR: THE MEETING OF THE MINDS

Even by doing all the ironing, however, a man cannot smooth out all the sources of incompatibility with a woman. At some point in the course of knowing each other, a romantic couple is expected to sustain a conversation that touches on political issues. This is bound to lead to disagreements, even on seemingly uncontroversial questions. Take legal aid. In British Columbia, we asked people whether they thought fellow citizens with low incomes should get access to free legal advice when involved in court cases. It's the kind of question that tends to prompt the answer "Yes." After all, most of us are kind people and our instinct is to sympathize when we're given the chance. But in the follow-up questions, we asked about specific kinds of legal advice and how important it was to put tax dollars towards them. At this point, a number of women said that, while free legal advice was very important in family court, it was only somewhat important in criminal cases. Meanwhile, a quarter of the men thought it only somewhat important for low-income people to get legal aid

"It's very important to have legal aid available for family court."

84%

69%

men

women

in family-related disputes such as divorces and child custody battles. Warning to men: This half-hearted attitude could ruin an otherwise pleasant dinner date.

Women would vote to keep the Canadian Senate and the one-cent coin. (Men would get rid of both.) They generally lend more support to smoking bans, and aren't as keen as men to scrap the gun registry. Women usually want to see the national flag in Ottawa lowered every time a Canadian soldier is killed, a less widespread view among men.

Half of the women in this country think police should do more roadside checks and speed traps, and they support photo radar in school zones and on highways, as well as remote-controlled cameras at intersections. These sorts of sneaky law enforcement tactics often strike men as totally unfair. A typical woman's sense of unfairness is provoked in a different way, however. She's more likely to respond to stories of unequal treatment. For instance, she feels really bothered when banks pay greater rates of interest to rich people who already have more money to invest in their GICs and savings accounts.

If this issue comes up, it might seem like a good idea for men to tell women that you can haggle with a bank to get a better rate on your GIC or RRSP deposits; banks don't advertise this point but it's often true. On the other hand, women tell us they dislike haggling and would rather not have to negotiate for a fair deal, so a man who insists on this point might not be perceived as being helpful.

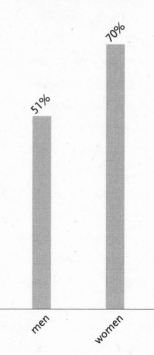

"I think it's unfair when banks reward the rich."

70%

51%

men

women

STEP FIVE: ACCEPTING DIFFERENCES

Let's imagine this Canadian man and woman have come a long way since they were necking in the car by the ocean all those years ago. Maybe she's got her job in the government (and now hankers after a career as a lounge singer instead), and maybe he's become a expert at buying appropriate gifts, using the steam iron, and chatting over dinner.

At some point, every successful relationship relies on compromise. The man and woman realize they can't just conform perfectly to each other's way of being, and must accept a few differences. Just as in the French language some objects are considered masculine and others feminine, so in the Canadian psyche there are things that belong in the male column and others that fit better in the female column. To make the task of compromising easier to manage, we've compiled a quick guide to some of the issues, traits, and common objects that generally belong to one gender more than the other. It's presented in the following easy-access list.

- Men are much more likely than women to name "other drivers" as presenting a major hazard on the roads.
- Women are twice as likely as men to say that sunshine and glare on the windshield present a hazard to driving. One in five female drivers name this as a major hazard, compared to just one in ten male drivers. (Complaints about the hazards of slippery roads also come more often from women.)
- Two out of every five Canadian men complain about their partner's habit of backseat driving. Two out of every five Canadian women admit to backseat driving regularly.
- Half of the men we spoke with admit to a weakness for mac-and-cheese. Only a third of Canadian women list this as a food they crave regularly. More women than men ate yogourt this week. Asked to choose which foodstuff would be impossible to

live without, more women picked chocolate than fruit. Only one woman out of a hundred chose peanut butter.

- Most men want a snack at bedtime. Most women don't. This week, more men than women will munch cookies. The number of Canadian men who ate cookies last week matches the number of Canadian women who ate yogourt. (Well, give or take a few, anyway.)
- Two out of five women feel guilty when they snack. Men are much less likely to feel this way. Women consider snacktime to be the hardest time to be healthy. Men say the hardest time is breakfast, when the unhealthy options are so much more appetizing. Most men say it'd be easier to eat healthily if healthy food tasted better. Women are equally divided on this issue.
- Men are more likely than women to complain that fresh vegetables aren't of such good quality during the winter months. They usually don't find it difficult to consume enough vegetables at this time of year. Women are more likely to notice the price of healthy foods going up. Most women find it harder to consume enough vegetables during the winter, and a quarter of women express this concern very strongly.
- Men generally don't have any concerns about the level of sodium in canned soups. A third of women avoid canned soups because of the high sodium content.
- Women who planned or hoped to celebrate Valentine's Day were asked to choose from the list below which creature best characterized their current or ideal romantic partner: cuddly bear, kitten, tiger, butterfly, stallion, swan, monkey, gorilla, bear, dog. (It probably won't surprise you to learn that we did this survey at the request of a well-known company that makes greeting cards.) The most popular answer from women was the cuddly bear.
- Men who planned or hoped to celebrate Valentine's Day were also asked to choose a creature from the list above. The most popular answer from Canadian men was "Don't know."

So, in conclusion, if your own relationship resembles one between a cuddly bear and a "Don't know," we hope that the five steps outlined earlier will go some way towards helping you understand each other better.

Weight and See

Finally, we can't leave the Canadian man and woman behind without an honest look at their physical appearance and what they think about it.

Women with jobs struggle especially hard with choosing what to wear. Find a group of ten women who work in Ontario and, as long as they're a diverse, representative bunch who reflect the province as a whole, one of those women will admit to you her constant difficulty finding clothes in her wardrobe that go well together—this despite the fact that she owns plenty of items. Four of the women will say they're bored with wearing the same things all the time, while another four won't sympathize much because they have no difficulties at all. One other woman will allude to some "other" clothing difficulty that refuses to be categorized. Two of the ten women will admit that part of the problem in their case is that none of their clothes seem to fit.

If you then sent the women out of the room and hunted down a group of ten representative men to ask them the same questions about fashion in the workplace, you'd find seven of them would look mystified and tell you this so-called "problem" has never occurred to them. Of the remaining three, two guys would admit they get a bit bored wearing the same things all the time. One of these two men might add that his clothes mostly don't match, don't fit, and so on. Finally, the one remaining guy would announce that he has a huge problem finding enough time to put a great outfit together every day.

Given an opportunity to complain about their co-workers' dress sense, two of the men and three of the women from these groups would willingly express a few criticisms. The most likely comments from the men would focus on how formally or casually people dress—they'd say their co-workers dress up or dress down too much. An equally common complaint from men is that their co-workers wear dirty or wrinkly clothes. Women don't make this last observation as often but they're even more picky about the formality of their colleagues' fashion choices, and are equally particular about any tendencies people have to dress inappropriately for their age.

When buying clothes or convenience items, nineteen out of twenty Canadians use their debit cards frequently, with women at the forefront of the debit-card revolution. Most women say they walk around with less cash in their pocket than they did a few years ago and 70% "always or usually use debit for purchases," compared to just 58% of men.

Almost all women, and most men too, say that a person's career growth and success is tied to their personal image. But when it comes to the shape of their bodies, Canadian women say their main reason for wanting to lose weight is for their own health and self-esteem. This is true even for those who already have a healthy body-mass index—most of these women also want to lose weight. In fact, a third of the women who are classified as medically *underweight* say they need to lose even more fat. A gap exists between what doctors consider "slightly overweight" and what many women think is overweight.

Sixty percent of women say that they feel a generalized social pressure to lose weight, and two-thirds think about their weight regularly. Most (56%) say they are outright fat, particularly those aged 35 to 54. Even among those aged 18 to 34, half of the women surveyed agreed with the statement, "I am fat."

Only one-fifth of Canadian women consider themselves to be at an ideal body weight.

Few women tell pollsters that their main reason for losing weight is to improve their image. By the way, for this survey we spoke with 2,365 women, and only 3 of them—that's 3 individual people, not 3%—said their main reason for wanting to lose weight was to please someone else. This number increased when we asked the survey respondents for their second-most-important reason for wanting to weigh less—122 women then told us it was because they wanted to "please others." Most of these people were young. In fact, 10% women aged 18 to 34 who want to lose weight list "pleasing others" as one of their top two reasons.

We also talked to men about their bodies. The guys in Alberta and Quebec were generally happy with their weight, while a majority of those in the rest of the country consider themselves a bit pudgy.

An interesting quirk in the answers to this question was that men who have kids at home tend to think their own body is just fine the way it is.

We also found out that guys with middle incomes of between $30,000 and $60,000 are the most confident in their bodies. Rich men consider themselves fat. A poorer man isn't more likely to describe his body as

"I'm a woman and I'm at least slightly overweight."

76%

62%

according to women surveyed

according to their doctors

overweight, but one out of every six will say he feels underweight rather than satisfied with his physique. One-third of the low-income men we spoke with say they worry about their body weight often or all the time. Wealthier guys don't spend as much time worrying. And interestingly, the men most likely to worry about their body size are the ones living in Alberta, where fewer people feel overweight. More than a third of Alberta men admit to worrying a great deal about this issue. Atlantic Canadian men commonly (40%) say they never think about their body mass, and they're the least likely to think other men are worrying about weight issues—only three out of ten believe this is a common worry, compared to four out of ten Alberta or Prairie men, who see the issue preying on the minds of other guys around them.

"I'm a man and I'm overweight."

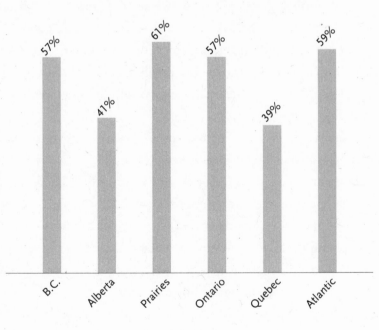

FEMALE SATISFACTION IN THE CITY

The HBO comedy/romance series *Sex and the City* showcased the lives and lifestyles of four smart, sophisticated New York women. The show gathered a massive female fan base as well as a number of guys who sat on the couch next to their partners . . . okay, for a little while before they went downstairs and turned on the History Channel.

Well, we decided to find out how satisfied urban women were in our own country—not just in the sex department but in a number of other areas as well. We spoke to women aged 25 to 64 in ten cities—Halifax, Quebec City, Montreal, Ottawa, Toronto, Hamilton, Winnipeg, Edmonton, Calgary, and Vancouver—about what made them satisfied in seven life areas.

A note of explanation about this particular survey: Sometimes, when we deal with really, really, sensitive topics, we don't want that pesky "margin of error" to get in the way of the results. For example, if you poll a limited group of people (we use the fancy term "discrete sample") the margin of error can be fairly big (you learned about this on page 10). Therefore, a finding based on a sample of 300 people can have a margin of error of +/- 5.8, which means that if the result appears to be 70%, it can actually be anywhere between 64.2% and 75.8%.

Let's say you're going to have a contest on a sensitive topic, like body image satisfaction, among a group of people you *never* want to upset—say, urban women in specific cities. (You are probably wondering: "What fool would ever attempt to do this? If the group of women in one city scored 70%, and the group of women in another city scored 69%, applying the margin of error would render the result a statistical tie! Wouldn't the respondents get really, really upset because there would be no clear cut winner?" Good question.)

Here's the answer with *the official language we are compelled to use*, and which by now you should all understand (if not, go back to page

10 and re-read it). We surveyed 2,102 Canadian women aged 25 to 64 in 10 major Canadian cities. The results of these polls were based on a sample that used quota sampling and weighting to balance the demographics and ensure that the sample's composition reflected that of the actual Canadian population according to Census data. Each city sample was then weighted to a comparable sample of 200. Respondents were then asked to assess their personal satisfaction in seven (7) life experience areas. Those respondents who indicated that they were "very satisfied" were assigned a vote weighting of 2 points; those who said they were "somewhat satisfied" were assigned a weighting of 1 point. The "votes" were then tallied to determine a category winner. Got it? No margin of error because these are points, or "votes," some deservedly worth more than others.

Boiled all down, here's what you'll see in the following two pages: The larger number on the bar chart (e.g., 236) is the total number of points or "votes." The smaller number (e.g., 112) is the number of points or "votes" garnered by women who said they were very satisfied. (And what are urban men most satisfied with? Sorry, they were all in the basement watching sports and the History Channel on TV. We'll get them next time they come upstairs and head for the fridge.)

As you can see, Toronto appears to be a clear winner. However, voting in some categories was very close.

MOST-SATISFIED WOMEN

- *satisfaction with themselves overall:* Toronto
- *satisfaction with their personal health:* Toronto
- *satisfaction with their personal body image:* Toronto
- *satisfaction with their love life:* Toronto
- *satisfaction with their friends and family:* Vancouver
- *satisfaction with their work:* Vancouver
- *satisfaction with their city overall:* Quebec City

Satisfaction with yourself overall

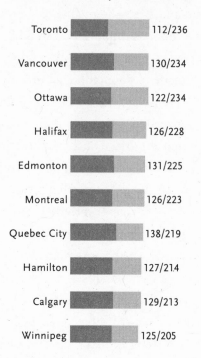

City	Score
Toronto	112/236
Vancouver	130/234
Ottawa	122/234
Halifax	126/228
Edmonton	131/225
Montreal	126/223
Quebec City	138/219
Hamilton	127/214
Calgary	129/213
Winnipeg	125/205

Satisfaction with your health

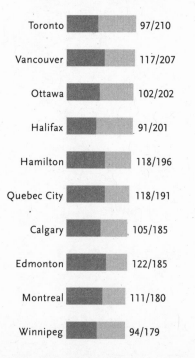

City	Score
Toronto	97/210
Vancouver	117/207
Ottawa	102/202
Halifax	91/201
Hamilton	118/196
Quebec City	118/191
Calgary	105/185
Edmonton	122/185
Montreal	111/180
Winnipeg	94/179

Satisfaction with your body image

City	Score
Toronto	95/159
Ottawa	88/155
Montreal	109/149
Edmonton	101/144
Vancouver	103/141
Quebec City	100/136
Halifax	99/134
Calgary	99/129
Hamilton	100/128
Winnipeg	87/126

Satisfaction with your love life

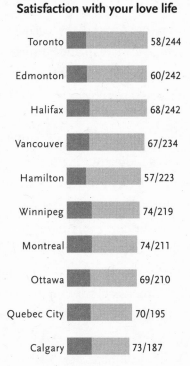

Toronto	58/244
Edmonton	60/242
Halifax	68/242
Vancouver	67/234
Hamilton	57/223
Winnipeg	74/219
Montreal	74/211
Ottawa	69/210
Quebec City	70/195
Calgary	73/187

Satisfaction with your relationships

Vancouver	79/297
Halifax	91/291
Winnipeg	84/288
Ottawa	88/282
Hamilton	82/281
Toronto	88/280
Calgary	91/275
Edmonton	103/270
Montreal	90/264
Quebec City	102/236

Satisfaction with your job

Vancouver	90/245
Edmonton	100/243
Calgary	86/238
Toronto	85/233
Halifax	91/233
Winnipeg	97/230
Ottawa	91/226
Hamilton	86/213
Montreal	98/213
Quebec City	111/204

Satisfaction with your city

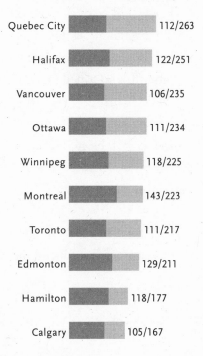

Quebec City	112/263
Halifax	122/251
Vancouver	106/235
Ottawa	111/234
Winnipeg	118/225
Montreal	143/223
Toronto	111/217
Edmonton	129/211
Hamilton	118/177
Calgary	105/167

The Ideal Mate

It appears that the ideal mate could be just around the corner, or maybe even next door. In fact, the average Canadian's ideal mate is not a tall bombshell model with gourmet chef skills and a sex drive that could melt ice, but rather one who possesses characteristics that could be classified as "average."

Interestingly, Canadian men and women appear to be suitably matched for each other, with both genders indicating that their ideal mates are similar. Both prefer similar attributes in their ideal mate, including average height and weight, enough money to get by, and enough cooking skills to avoid microwave dinners every night.

Both men and women agree that their ideal mate would be well informed about what is happening in the world—perhaps so that the conversation doesn't become dull. More specifically, eight in ten women (86%) and men (80%) say that their ideal mate would read at least one newspaper every day.

If the average Canadian could find their ideal mate, here's what the mate would look like:

- They would be of average height (66% prefer this)—rather than tall (29%) or short (6%).
- They would weigh an average amount (78% prefer this)—rather than buff and toned (12%), with love handles (9%), or lots to handle (1%).
- Their hair would be brown (38% prefer this)—not sandy (21%), black (19%), blond (15%), red (7%), or purple (less than 1%).
- Their eyes would be blue (43%)—not brown (22%), hazel (18%), green (15%), or black (2%).

For kicks, this ideal couple would spend their time near fireplaces, on romantic walks, sitting on beaches, and lighting candles (43%).

Less ideal couples—wait, we mean less "average" couples—prefer adventure, travel, discovery, museums, and history (24%), the outdoors, camping, hiking, sports, and fitness (18%); or entertainment, restaurants, nightlife, and theatre (16%).

As far as sex, most Canadians would choose a mate who is "warm" (69%). Only 30% want "scorching" lovers and only 1% want "cool" ones. Less than 1% chose "ice" as the word that best describes their ideal lover's sexual appetite.

As for money, most people would choose ideal mates with a "good" income (59%), compared with the quarter of people who want a mate who's "well off," or who lives on cash "as it comes" (15%). One out of a hundred Canadians express the lowest expectations and say their ideal mate would have money only "if it comes in."

Almost all respondents (96%) want the kind of decision-making relationship in which both partners would make decisions together. Just 2% would like their ideal mate to simply "call the shots, and I'd leave it to my love." At the opposite end of the scale, 2% would like to "call the shots" because they know what's best.

In terms of attitude towards domestic duties, the consensus was that the ideal mate would simply "do what is needed" (70%). Twenty-five percent would want their ideal mate to be "neat and tiny, spic and span"; 5% say that their ideal mate would want to "hire a maid"; and only 2% want a mate with a "Who cares?" attitude about domestic duties.

When it comes to the ideal personality, most Canadians (57%) would choose a partner with all-round personality. This is in contrast to those who would choose a mate whose is humorous (12%), upbeat/optimistic (11%), caring (10%), thoughtful (8%), or serious (2%).

And when single Canadians go to a party, they're most keen to chat up someone who peruses all the sections of an online or print newspaper (30%) rather than those bozos who read only the news and commentary sections (27%), the arts and lifestyles sections (17%), the sports section (8%), or the business section (3%). Fifteen percent would prefer their ideal mate not to have looked at any of the sections of an online or print newspaper.

Now, whether ideal or not, we're just pleased as punch to report that three-quarters of Canadians are involved in some kind of relationship—whether that be marriage (formal or common-law), partnership, or boyfriend/girlfriend (or "other," whatever that is). Some of these couples have secret dreams of how their love life could be more ideal, however. We asked Canadians "What do you dream about that you hide from your spouse?" The number-one response? Travelling with them (38%). Other popular answers: living somewhere else (17%), starting over in a different career (17%), travelling on your own (14%), living on your own for a while (9%), having an extramarital affair (8%), adopting a child (6%), or having plastic surgery (4%).

THE INFIDELS

Do Canadians cheat? (And we don't mean at cards.) For the record, we have been asking this question now in about every imaginable way on behalf of different organizations, mostly for newspapers and magazines, for roughly twenty years, and—this will perhaps be surprising to some people—the numbers never really change. This means one of two things: either everybody is telling the truth or everybody is lying. And, frankly, there's a lot more evidence to suggest that people are telling the truth. It also depends on what part of their lives these people are talking about.

You are far more likely to be cheated on or to cheat on your partner *before you are married*. Thirty-three percent of men and 35% of women indicate that before they reached the altar or obtained the civic licence, they were cheated on in a relationship. Younger people are more likely (40%) to say they have been cheated on than middle-aged (34%) or older Canadians (27%). If you live in Quebec, you are the least likely to have been cheated on. If you live in British Columbia, on the other hand, the chances are very high (42%).

No matter how many times we've asked this question, as discreetly or as overtly as possible, we end up with about 10% of Canadians currently married, divorced, separated, or living common-law admitting that they have had or are having an extramarital affair, and 6% of Canadians who have not had an affair say that they are likely to have one in the future. And to close the stereotype loop, yes, men are twice as likely (10%) as women (5%) to say that they would have an affair.

We even asked Canadians to imagine a handsome/beautiful alien dropping down out of the sky in perfect human anatomical dimensions and proportions. Try this yourself—got the image? Next, imagine that you happened to meet this character walking by a hotel room and he/she asked for sex. Would you go in and partake of this intergalactic experience? The answers we got were exactly the same as if a strictly human experience was offered up.

Here are some interesting tidbits that all of you current or aspiring couples should digest.

- *19% of married Canadians between the ages of 35 and 54 wish they could wake up one morning and discover that they were single.*
- *85% of all marriages, regardless of respondents' age, are "happy."*
- *The province where you are most likely to have your heart broken in any kind of relationship is Saskatchewan. The least likely is Quebec.*
- *Those in British Columbia and Ontario (9%) are more likely to expect to cheat on their partner, whereas Atlantic Canadians (3%) appear to be the most inclined to be faithful.*
- *The number-one reason given for having had an affair is loneliness. The second-most-popular reason is either "sex" or "love."*
- *29% of men say that they would have an affair just for sex, compared to 8% of women. Thirty percent of Canadians who have never been married say they would have an affair for sex.*

- *Roughly half of the respondents would forgive an affair (48% of women, 56% of men). The others would sever the relationship. The younger the person, the more likely it's going to be "Hasta la vista, baby!"*

ONE LAST WORD ON THSE FISH AND BICYCLE THING

We decided to investigate Canadian opinions on whether women generally need men more or less than fish need bicycles. Here's the breakdown by province.

"Women need men more than fish need bicycles."

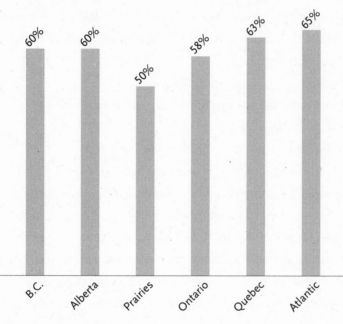

11 / THE BIG EARNER

It's not very polite to ask somebody how much money they earn. (FYI: For the same reason, it's also impolite to ask a rancher how many cattle he or she keeps, or to ask a sheep-farmer about the size of his or her flock.) Luckily, in our line of work, we're expected to be rude. In this chapter you'll find out where you fit into the ranks of Canadians rich and poor.

The fundamental truth is that the world will always welcome money. Sure, life throws challenges at everybody, whether it's disease, malnutrition, driver's tests, the difficulty of finding and keeping a job, the sorrow of lost love, a conflict with rivals, a complaint from the neighbours, or the many frustrations involved in maintaining a lawn or improving one's golf swing. A person's ability to meet these challenges, and the effect they have on that person's self-esteem, beliefs, and general outlook on life, depends a lot on the size of their money-pot. With a paycheque for $100,000 coming your way, overcoming an illness obviously looks different than it does if you're down to your last dime with the credit cards already maxed out.

That's why, when we ask people to give us their opinions on the big issues of the day or the smaller issues of daily life, we also (as politely as possible) get them to tell us their approximate yearly income, so we can compare rich with poor. Most of the time we call people "higher-income" if they live in households that take in more than $60,000 a year. Households with incomes between $30,000 and $60,000 are in the middle, while those earning less than $30,000 per year are considered "low-income." It's true that we'd find interesting opinions among the very rich, who may live altogether different lives on their $250,000 annual take and therefore disagree with the higher-income people scraping by on merely $65,000 a year . . . but sadly we can't give very rich people their own voice on every issue we investigate because there simply aren't enough of these folks to show up in the average sample—when we want to ask them questions, we have to make a special effort to seek them out.

To make this point, we went to the great temple of Canadian statistics known as Statistics Canada (now that's a novel name, and so typically Canadian), and we discerned the following interesting factoids based on the 2006 Census:

- Out of the 24,113,140 Canadian adults over the age of eighteen, 5,483,130 earn $50,000 or more in a year.

Among that group, you'll find:

- 2,304,580 Canadians who earn $75,000 or more
- 1,048,510 Canadians who earn $100,000 or more
- 389,620 Canadians who earn $150,000 or more
- 180,650 Canadians who earn $200,000 or more
- 144,870 Canadians who earn $250,000 or more

Meanwhile, the average after-tax earnings of an unattached Canadian are less than $30,000 a year.

So, when we look at those people who we consider "upper income," those who earn more than $60,000 a year, they represents approximately 16% of the Canadian public, or one in six Canadians. Less than 1% of Canadians (0.6%, to be exact) earn $250,000 or more. That's why we don't poll the group in big enough numbers to find out what they're thinking. (We hope any extremely wealthy people reading this book won't suffer from feelings of exclusion and neglect.)

Is a Hundred Grand "Rich"?

People who have at least $100,000 in financial assets (this doesn't include their home or the land it's on, or their jewellery or their collection of Andy Warhol prints) are the cash-richest fifth of Canadians. But very few of them think they're wealthy—95% say they're not.

PLANS FOR RETIREMENT

The high-income earner doesn't want to retire downtown. Middle-income Canadians divide equally on the question. Poorer Canadians think it'd be great to retire to a downtown home with easy access to arts, cultural activities, restaurants, entertainment venues, and sporting events.

The most surprising thing about people's retirement plans, however, is how similar they are regardless of income. A home close to nature appeals to roughly the same proportion of wealthy Canadians as poorer ones (about 85% to 90%). A condominium community finds slightly more fans among low-income Canadians (64% like the idea) than high-income earners (57%), but that's nothing like the difference between, say, British Columbians (half of whom hate the idea) and Albertans (three-quarters say they'd like to retire this way).

Generally, wealthier people say they're drawn to retire somewhere where young people also live, where their home is well suited to entertaining family and friends, and where they don't have to house an elderly relative. Lower-income Canadians express enthusiasm for the latter option, particularly a home that contains separate living quarters for the aged, what the British call a "granny flat."

Higher-income people don't like high-rises. Seventy percent wouldn't want to retire to one, even if it included a concierge service, a health club, a pool, and a maid. A slight majority (55%) of low-income Canadians also find this a less appealing option.

The wealthier set plan to remodel their homes in retirement, at least in some minor way. Most lower-income people do not. Those in higher, lower, and every income level in between are equally likely to move closer to their families—roughly a third expect this. Wealthier people are extremely unlikely to move to a larger home when they retire (perhaps because they already live in big place). Only 7% see this in their future, while roughly half expect to downsize. Upsizing is much more popular among lower-income Canadians—one-fifth of Baby Boomers who aren't earning much right now hope to move into a bigger home upon retiring. One-third plan to live in something smaller.

HOW DID THEY GET SO RICH?

On the face of it, it sounds as though only a tiny portion of wealthy people started life in a rich family. In fact, 97% of people who own real estate valued at more than half a million dollars describe their upbringing as less than "wealthy or affluent." That creates a remarkable view of the country, with all those hard-working, goal-oriented people rising to the top so quickly.

Of course, the other possibility is that people always think of themselves as middle class. Roughly 94% of wealthy homeowners describe their upbringing this way—15% call it upper middle class, 48% say it was plain middle, and 31% say they grew up in the lower middle class. Just 4% of people who own expensive homes tell us they grew up in poverty.

When we ask rich people—in this case, those with property assets worth over half a million dollars—how they got established financially, here's what we hear:

- 4% were born into the right family.
- 1% got there by luck.

- 27% benefited mainly from a drive to succeed.
- 18% relied on a good education.
- 46% credit their own hard work.
- 4% point to some other reason.

How wealthy homeowners describe their upbringing:

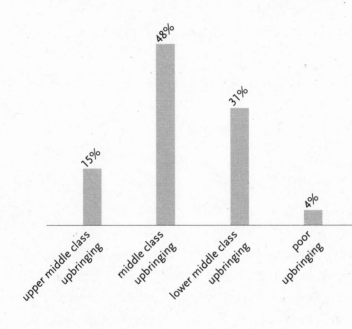

THE COLLEGE TEST

As we'll see in the next chapter, Canadians intuitively believe that time spent at university is a good investment for a young adult. The rewards for that investment might be a long time coming, however, and in the meantime the recent graduates need to start paying off their debts—the average student builds up a $25,000 debt during four years of undergraduate school.

Adults seem to disagree on how much tuition costs, depending on how much they earn themselves:

**How much would you guess a student pays
for one year's tuition in your province?**

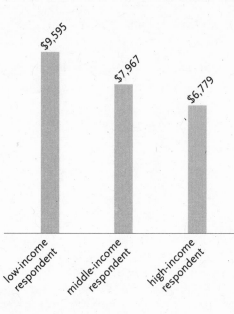

In case you're wondering about this one, the *actual* average tuition fee for a full-time Canadian student was $4,347 when we got these answers (at the end of 2007). That's not including books and keg parties. You might say that the guesses above were almost spot on if the low-income people were thinking of the cost for medical students, while the middle-income group imagined law students, and the high-earners were talking about Nova Scotia, where the average tuition has crept up to $6,600. Quebec students pay $2,000. Most other provinces' schools charge $5,000 on average. Wannabe dentists pay $13,463.

OFF TO SCHOOL?

Most rural families say that university tuition is now too expensive for anyone in their household to consider higher education. In fact, only 23% of rural people say that tuition costs do not prevent them or their kids from going to university.

By the way, city families don't escape this problem with their higher-income urban jobs. Two-thirds of Edmontonians, and roughly 60% of people in Toronto, Calgary, Vancouver, and Ottawa, agree that post-secondary school costs are simply too high for them to afford. Montreal is the exception—just 43% agree that tuition costs make higher education impossible for them.

The average starting income for a university graduate is slightly over $30,000 (the kids who didn't go to college are actually out-earning them at this point). With this in mind, more-moneyed or higher-income people figure $17,400 is a reasonable debt for a student to carry. One in eight lower-income people say "no debt at all" is the only reasonable amount, and a further quarter of them think student debts should never surpass $10,000. On average, though, people who earn under $30,000 per year say it's reasonable for a student to graduate in debt to the tune of half a year's income: $14,445. All of these suggestions, remember, amount to much less than the typical debt in real life, despite the fact that most of us overestimate the price of tuition.

THOUGHT EXPERIMENT

If you ask a random (for our purposes, "random" here means "perfectly representing the whole Canadian population") think-tank of ten high-income Canadians about what the government should make its first priority in a higher education policy, four of them will demand a guarantee of university or college spaces for every qualified student. Only one of these wealthier people would think the biggest priority is to ensure access for students from groups currently under-represented in universities. If you could, by magic or trickery, turn these people instantly into ten poor Canadians with incomes under $30,000 a year, one of them would abandon that demand for a broad guarantee and join forces with the person calling for better access for the outsider groups.

Maybe that sounds anticlimactic. Okay. Let's imagine the think tank has a million people. Now one hundred thousand folks are making the same move, calling for a focus on marginalized people!

THE COMMUTING QUESTION

If you earn less than $30,000 a year . . .
Chances are you don't commute to work because you're either retired, unemployed, or you generally work from home. If you do commute, your job site, office, or other workplace is less than 5 kilometres away.

If you earn between $30,000 and $60,000 . . .
You're equally likely to work from home, travel less than 10 kilometres to work, or endure a longer commute. If you commute, you drive.

If you earn over $60,000 . . .
You probably commute. If so, the trip is likely to be longer than 10 kilometres. You drive.

- 80% of high-income Canadians commute to work every day.
- Two-thirds of middle income people do.
- 40% of low-income Canadians commute to work.

Among those who commute:
- 60% of low-income workers travel less than 5 kilometres.
- Roughly half of middle-income workers travel under 10 kilometres.
- 57% of big earners travel more than 10 kilometres.

Gas pumps up the pedestrians

In the final years of the Bush presidency (#43—you know, the son of #41—also known as "Dubya"), a sharp rise in gas prices in North America prompted many commuters to change their habits. The ones who responded the quickest to higher fuel costs were those workers with low incomes (who also usually have shorter commutes). More than half of these people walked to work more often. One-third relied more on public transit. A quarter even moved house, choosing a residence closer to their job.

Higher-income workers also responded, but differently. Hardly any moved house, but many bought vehicles that offered better mileage. In fact, more high-income workers in Canada bought or used a new vehicle than switched to public transit.

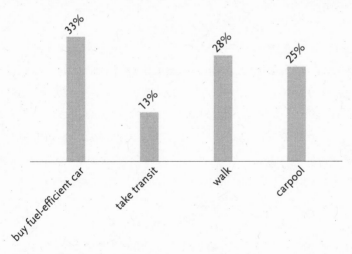

"I'm a high-income Canadian who commutes to work. When gas prices get too high for too long, I change my habits in the following way . . ."

And even though the price at the pumps dropped when the price of oil went from around US$150 a barrel to US$40 a barrel, the recession that followed discouraged Canadians from going back to old habits. In many ways, new behaviours had already become ingrained.

Strangely enough, one in twenty middle-income workers tell us that they commute to work using some form of transport other than bus, train, car, bike, or walking.

THE NEWS QUESTION

People with big incomes are slightly more likely to trust the traditional news media, such as newspapers, news magazines, and TV and radio news programs. Seventy-two percent express at least a "fair amount" of trust, compared to two-thirds of low-income Canadians. But whereas most people living on a small income believe the news media's primary goal is to find and broadcast the truth, the group with bigger paycheques isn't so sure. Half of them say the media's first goal is really to run a business and make money. Incidentally, one in eight wealthy Canadians would discourage their child from becoming a journalist.

HELP WITH CAREER PATH

The Internet helps lower-income earners more directly than higher-income earners. Most people with household incomes under $60,000 have used an online support or networking group at some point to find a job or get career advice. Most people earning over $60,000 have not. The bigger earners often credit co-workers and associates with helping them on their career path—roughly three-quarters mention a helpful colleague as an important factor in their current success. Just 59% of lower-income Canadians have received useful career help from a colleague or business associate. That's about the same proportion who credit government employment centres or a community job agency. If you bring in more than $60,000, you probably haven't used the latter (only one in three big earners say they have).

Low-income Canadians . . .

- who at some point saw a career specialist or school guidance counsellor often (48%) describe these people as helpful.
- think they'd benefit from having their own career coach to help them improve their resumés and perform better in interviews.
- often regret not getting professional career advice (45%).
- are twice as likely as rich people to "wish my parents had backed off and given me more freedom to choose my own career" (20% say this).
- usually don't have to deal with office politics.

High-income Canadians . . .

- are less likely (37%) to say their guidance counsellor or career coach was helpful.
- don't regret not getting career advice.
- hardly ever say that parents should "just leave it up to the school to help children choose their careers."
- complain about office politics detracting from their ability to do their jobs properly.

Fifty-three percent of people earning between $80,000 and $100,000 say that office politics "get in the way" of their work. Thirty-one percent of people who earn under $40,000 have the same complaint. Just 23% of people who earn over $100,000 say office politics don't cause them much hassle at all.

You Earn What You Eat

Most people with large incomes don't skip meals as frequently as less-well-off people. Half of low-income Canadians regularly skip breakfast. Sixty-two percent of people earning $60,000 or more don't. Forty percent of people earning less than $60,000 say their typical snacks are generally becoming less healthy. Seventy percent of people on higher incomes say, for them, this isn't true. Only one-fifth of big earners confess to snacking more often than they used to due to time constraints. One-third of people on lower incomes say they are doing this.

Snacks eaten more commonly in low-income households: muffins, donuts. Snacks eaten more commonly in households of over $60,000: candy or chocolate, fruit, cheese and crackers.

The Single Issue

If you live in a low-income household, you're probably single, divorced, separated, or widowed. Most middle-income Canadians are either married or living common-law. Most better-off Canadians (67%) are married.

A low-income person usually lives alone or with one other person. A high-income individual typically lives in a household of at least three people. Half of these Canadians have a child under 18 years old. Just under half of middle-income people share a home with three others. One in five middle-income people live alone.

- -

ROMANTIC VACATIONS
- Higher-income couples escape on holidays together without their kids. Eighty percent have taken such a trip in the last five years.

- Half of low-income couples have not shared a vacation (without kids) for more than five years. In fact, 34% say they've never taken a vacation together as a couple.
- Two-thirds of middle-income couples have vacationed without children in the last five years.

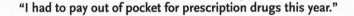

WAITING, WAITING, WAITING

However much money a person makes, he or she is bound to say that long waits for hospital treatment are a problem. But people come up with different explanations for the waits. Moneyed people (70%) say it's a lack of resources. Poor people tend to say they just don't know why the waiting times have to be so long—one in eight express this feeling, which you'll hardly ever hear from people with bigger incomes.

"I had to pay out of pocket for prescription drugs this year."

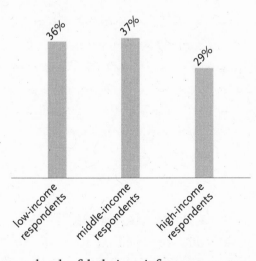

Among the people who felt their wait for treatment was unreasonably long, the wealthier ones twice as often describe feelings of frustration as the main consequence. Lower-income Canadians are more likely to say the main effect of long waits was that their medical condition got worse.

WHERE'S THE MONEY?

A quarter of Canadian households with over $60,000 per year are in the greater Toronto area. Just 10% of households earning less than this share this area. Three out of ten low-income Canadians live in Quebec. Roughly the same portion lives west of Ontario, but western Canada is also home to a third of the country's high-earners, while Quebec is home to only one out of six such wealthy households (many in Montreal). More well-to-do people live in Toronto than in all of Quebec.

Sixty-one percent of Canadians in low-income households are women. Fifty-six percent of Canadians in high-income households are men. Middle-income Canadian households are split, suitably enough, right down the middle—half men, half women.

Half of the big earners are middle-aged, between 35 and 54 years old. Just a quarter of the people in households earning under $30,000 are in this age group. (Forty percent of poorer Canadian adults are seniors; one-third are under 35.)

HOW OLD ARE MILLIONAIRES?

Most Canadian millionaires are retired. Their average age is 61.5 (so now is a good time to start planning what to buy the average millionaire for his 62nd birthday). One in three have a household income under $100,000. One in six are under the age of 45. Half of them own more than one piece of real estate.

IS A PENNY SAVED A PENNY BURNED?

The recent economic downturn and big losses in the RRSP/mutual fund markets caused Boomers to seriously reconsider when to hang up their work clothes.

Because of the effect of the global economic meltdown on their retirement savings, 28% of Boomers told us they plan on delaying the date of their retirement, either by 1 to 2 years (43%) or 3 to 5 years (37%), although some are delaying it for 5 or more years (9%). Just 3% will delay their retirement for less than a year.

It appears that the economic slump has had an even greater effect on the anticipated retirement dates for Boomers who own businesses and had been planning to retire within the next 5 years; 37% indicate that they will delay their retirement. But then again, many retiring Boomers who own businesses (32%) will never really fully retire—a full 19 points higher than the proportion of Boomers overall who say they will keep working. Thinking ahead to when they're 65 years old, 50% of Boomers who own businesses think they'll be only semi-retired or working part-time, compared to 40% of Boomers overall who think that this will be the case. Furthermore, 37% of Boomers who own their own businesses expect to be fully retired at age 65, compared to 47% of Boomers overall who think they'll be in this position.

If they had enough money to retire, 25% of Boomers overall would do so right away, compared to 18% of retiring Boomers who own businesses. Fifty percent of Boomers overall would work part-time or occasionally (versus 54% of retiring business owners), and 25% would continue to work full-time despite having enough money to retire (versus 28% of retiring business owners).

So if some Boomers are looking at bust, what about the broader Canadian population and their overall mood regarding their retirement savings? Well, many Canadians (44%) have been describing their mood as "steady," understanding that "the market has its ups and downs, and that it will get back on track and make up any losses so far." A sizable chunk of Canadians (32%) told us they felt "fine" and that they "don't think about what happened, and don't have any worries."

But a quarter of Canadians couldn't bring themselves to express such confidence about their retirement savings. Nineteen percent described feelings of anxiety and concern that caused them to "do some revisions to my investments and life plans." Five percent were in full-on "panic" mode and, as the recession deepened, said, "I'm doing everything I can to salvage our life savings."

CANADIANS AND THEIR BANKING HABITS

Economic fallout made us feel especially grumpy about paying banking charges. Here's what we heard from Canadians as the markets tumbled:

- 65% pay more attention to service fees. Canadians say they pay $14.30 in total for service fees on their main personal chequing account in an average month. Of those who have a chequing account, 32% pay less than $10 in an average month. Thirty-three percent pay between $10 and $20, while a further 12% pay fees of $21 or more. Twenty-three percent are unsure of their average monthly fees.
- 62% are more likely to open a tax-free savings account.
- 51% plan to put more money into that savings account.
- 59% are actively looking for ways to reduce service fees.
- 56% will save more in case they and/or another wage-earner in the household loses a job.
- 52% have changed or plan to change how financial transactions are conducted to reduce service fees.
- 49% have invested or plan to invest more in a high-interest savings account instead of other investments that tend to be more heavily impacted by market conditions.
- 43% have reduced or plan to reduce the number of financial transactions they conduct to reduce service fees.
- 40% will save more in order to make up for losses already experienced by investments due to current economic conditions.
- 35% have invested or plan to invest more in a regular savings account instead of other investments that tend to be more heavily impacted by market conditions.

- 32% have invested or plan to invest more in term deposits or GICs instead of other investments that tend to be more heavily impacted by market conditions.

RAINY DAY INTEREST?

Despite this high level of willingness to save and invest money, the amount saved for a rainy day by the average Canadian tends to be fairly small. Fifty-three percent of all those who save for emergencies or "just in case" situations have less than $5,000 in savings. One in five have savings valued between $5,000 and $9,999, and one in ten have savings valued between $10,000 and $24,999. Only 6% have savings of $25,000 and upwards. The remaining 12% of respondents are either unsure or uncomfortable answering this question.

Fifty-four percent of savings account owners are dissatisfied with the interest rate earned by their primary account. On the other hand, 41% are satisfied with their current interest rate, and 5% are unsure how they feel. A higher interest rate would likely encourage Canadians to save more money. Three-quarters of Canadians agree with the statement "If savings accounts offered higher interest rates, it would encourage me to save more money than I do right now." Still, a sizable minority (19%) disagree, and the remaining 6% are unsure of the impact of a higher interest rate.

SO, AFTER TRYING TO KEEP TRACK OF THAT MONEY FOR SO LONG, THEN WHAT?

Answer: Fuggettaboutit.

It appears that many Canadian retirees aren't keeping track of their expenditures as they adjust to their new lifestyle, with 76% indicating that they don't know how much money they spent during the first year of their retirement. Among the quarter who do know, 46% say they spent more than they expected, while only 12% said they spent less. Forty-two percent of retirees, however, had had no expectations about what they would spend during their first year of retirement.

Unexpected costs catch 39% of Canadian retirees off guard. The most commonly cited unexpected costs include home repairs or maintenance (45%), health care costs for themselves or their spouse (42%), vehicle repairs (36%), a new vehicle (28%), a child or grandchild moving back in (23%), health care for a parent (4%), or some other expense (26%).

Three-quarters of retirees made large purchases within the first three years of retirement. Topping the list of purchases were a trip (41%), a car (38%), home improvements (37%), or home maintenance (20%). But average retirees spend most of their money (58%) on day-to-day living expenses, followed by health care costs (10%), treating themselves (9%), treating their family (8%), supporting their family (8%), and other expenses (8%).

Those who have not yet retired expect to have a slightly different budget makeup, allocating about half of their annual spending to day-to-day expenditures, 14% to treating themselves, 12% to health care, 10% to supporting their family, 10% to treating their family, and 8% to other expenses.

ACQUIRING A WEALTHY MINDSET

If you're a commuter who knows the cost of university tuition, shuns downtown retirements, chose a career without help from the Internet, generally trusts the news media despite their profit motive, finds office politics frustrating, and enjoys a happy marriage full of romantic getaways, you're probably rich. If you fit into all those categories but still aren't rich, you clearly have a wealthy mindset, which could be either a good thing or a dangerous thing for somebody on a lower income!

Some of the people who fit the "low-income household" category are hoping to earn much more money later on, however, because they're currently university students who expect to snag a great career someday. While they might share some concerns with older people on small incomes, their general outlook on life is bound to be different, as are their responses to important personal and political questions. In fact, as soon as a person enrols in a course at a post-secondary school, he or she has entered a new category for opinion pollsters. We've noticed plenty of ways in which time spent in higher education seems to relate to the way people answer the questions we ask. That's the topic of our next chapter.

12 / THE SCHOLAR

Considering that many Canadians believe people soon forget what they learned in university, it's amazing how solidly we stand together in encouraging young people to stay in school as long as possible. Ninety-nine percent of parents think it's important that grade schools build the skills a child needs to attend college or university, making this one of the most uncontroversial opinions in Canada. (The figure drops to 97% in Quebec, rendering it only as uncontroversial as the belief that Elvis Presley has died.) Once a young person becomes eligible to attend college or university, he or she would be rejecting the advice of 93% of adults in deciding not to go.

What's so great about all this higher learning? Two out of five Albertans figure you won't remember much of what you learn in university—a judgment that probably refers to the scholarly information rather than to the more memorable keg parties, dorm-room romances, and so on. Even Albertans agree, however, that attending university has a huge impact on a person's life. Only in Quebec did we find many people who didn't think attending places of higher learning would have much effect on their future.

"I don't think attending university really has such a huge impact on a person's life."

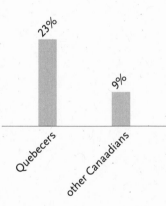

A university degree gives a person a better chance of obtaining a more satisfying and higher-paying job, say the vast majority of Canadians. And many people argue attending university has other effects . . .

- A quarter of university graduates think higher education makes you less religious.
- A quarter of Canadians think universities corrupt young people by filling them with left-wing beliefs.
- A quarter of Canadians think people with university educations have a better sense of right and wrong when it comes to tricky moral questions.
- One in ten university graduates believe people with more formal education should be given more voting power in elections than those with less education.

Beer Review

The more formal education you have, the more likely you are to have cracked open a beer this month. Here's a list of who drinks at least one beer in any given four-week period:
- 60% of university graduates
- 55% of people with some post-secondary schooling
- 49% of high school graduates
- 48% of high school dropouts

And here's a look at who chugs two beers or more per week:
- 24% of university graduates
- 19% of people with some post-secondary schooling
- 18% of high school graduates
- 16% of high school dropouts

Belonging to a Nation

People with little formal education claim allegiance to their town or province (53%) more often than they claim allegiance to their country (33%). University grads tend to feel a sense of belonging to Canada more than to their region or town. Whereas people who didn't finish high school are very unlikely to say they belong first and foremost to "the world," this idea is fairly popular among university grads—12% say they're global citizens first, national citizens second.

Almost everyone without secondary education believes Canada's success as a society depends on the idea that we all share a common history, common heroes, and national symbols. That sounds suspect to many people with university educations. Although a majority do agree with this sentiment—six in ten—38% beg to differ, arguing that Canada's strength actually comes from the fact that we *don't* have a national culture, so people aren't expected to conform to one set of rules. Maybe this explains why people with university degrees don't have a problem with the idea of dual citizenship. It's controversial among high school grads, 43% of whom think a person should make up his or her mind and commit to being solely a Canadian citizen. University graduates mostly approve of keeping one foot in another country, so to speak.

What brings everyone together, apparently, is the beaver. Regardless of how much time a person has spent in school, they're equally likely to feel a bond with the little animal, as well as with the maple leaf, the Mountie, the canoe, and hockey.

Just 'Cause

Asking people what they think, what they've done with their lives, what experiences they've had, etc., and then comparing their answers can reveal a ton of interesting coincidences. Like the fact that university grads are more likely to get their hearts broken.

The stats don't lie—going to college or university raises your chances of getting dumped by e-mail, by telephone, by a handwritten letter, or in person, whether at a bar or restaurant, in the open air, or at home. So if you want to avoid a nasty breakup, a good move is to drop out of high school before you collect a diploma, right?

Hmm . . . it's a neat idea. We might get in trouble, however, for drawing a conclusion like that one. While it's fun to speculate about why heartbreak and formal education could relate, we haven't actually proved a real connection. After all, university grads drink beer more regularly, and they're also much more likely to have witnessed a butterfly emerge from its pupa. Does beer drinking or butterfly watching lead to romantic breakup? People with college educations report being happier in their jobs; it doesn't seem very likely that job satisfaction makes a person more likely to get dumped by telephone!

Opinion polls help a scientist track all kinds of root causes for what happens in society. It's a difficult task that requires a careful professional who can reflect soberly on the facts. Leaping to conclusions isn't really part of the job.

But that shouldn't ruin all the fun of noticing the odd matches that society offers up. Even if what looks like an interesting connection turns out to be misleading—maybe getting dumped isn't caused directly by going to college—it's still a great way to prompt the imagination and draw attention to new ways of seeing our lives.

How to Be Old

When people hit retirement age, their life choices still bear the stamp of the kind of formal education they received. Let's assume hopefully for a moment that most Boomers (including this book's two authors) will find their way past the RRSP losses they recently suffered. This being the case, two-thirds of Boomers with a high school diploma plan to stay put where they currently live. Half of university graduates expect to move. Among those who anticipate living somewhere else after retirement, one-quarter of university graduates would most prefer a "cultural or arts" community focused on heritage, learning, music, and ideas. This appeals to only a handful of high school graduates, who are usually drawn more to a "health," "social," or "nature" community focused on fitness, social events, or outdoor activities. Among Boomers hoping to move after retirement, the idea of a community close to nature, where they can spend time hiking, boating, skiing, and fishing, appeals strongly to 38% of people with a high school education or less. Only a quarter of those with a college or university degree put this at the top of their wish list.

These differences may not seem surprising—after all, many university departments do their best to fill students' heads with a love of art, music, and learning, so it makes sense that these interests would affect their retirement dreams. Some of the effects of higher education, however, seem a bit weirder. For example, how close does a retiring Boomer want to live to his or her parents?

Surely, along with all those highfalutin concepts about art and culture, students aren't being taught to keep a safe distance from their aging parents? And yet it would seem that holding a university degree is at least indirectly connected to the idea that a retirement home shared with elderly parents or relatives is an unappealing prospect.

Twenty percent of high school dropouts say the one foodstuff they absolutely could not go without is meat. Only 7% of university graduates say this.

Here's another morsel for thought: Boomers who eschewed formal education after high school overwhelmingly want to retire to a community with other people of a similar age. Nearly three-quarters find this prospect appealing. People with university degrees, on the other hand, often don't go for that standard retirement community image. They're split 50/50 on whether such a place would be desirable.

Retirement means more hours in the day for odd jobs such as fixing a cracked chimney, replacing old knob-and-tube wiring, or perhaps putting in a new bathtub. In fact, ambitious retirees could spend their time restoring or updating an antique home as a project—something that might pay for itself when the work is completed. Sound appealing? It does to many Boomers who didn't complete high school: 42% would happily take on such a retirement project. Ask the university graduates, however, and they'll probably shake their heads. Three-quarters of them say that taking on an antique fixer-upper at that stage of life sounds like a terrible idea!

"When I retire, I'd like a home with separate living quarters designed to meet the needs of aging, elderly, or infirm parents or relatives."

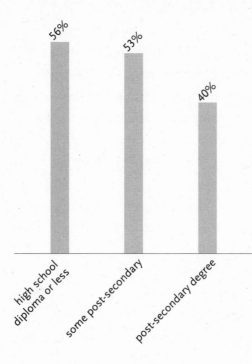

What to Think about God

University graduates are more careful about the messages put out by religious groups. Whereas 41% of people whose formal education stopped short of post-secondary schools think that religious groups make a pretty good contribution to public debate, 70% of university graduates think the contribution is poor or terrible.

Only 13% of university graduates say they don't believe in God, but that still makes them twice as likely to be atheists. The more education a person has, the greater the chance that they think university attendance makes people less religious—a quarter of Canadians with degrees believe this. In Ontario and Quebec, 20% think universities make students become less religious. Half of the Albertans and Atlantic Canadians we spoke to disagreed with this idea very strongly. Overall, so did half of the women in Canada.

How to Handle Money

Half of the people who didn't finish high school grew up without anyone they consider particularly influential to teach them to save money. One-quarter say their mother taught them to save. Only 13% mention their father as the main influence in good money management. Among university graduates, one-quarter say it was dad who influenced their financial habits; one-quarter say it was mom; one-quarter say it was professionals, friends, or spouses; and the remaining quarter said no-one had an influence.

Among high school graduates who took their education no further, half say their family encouraged saving. Ten percent were taught to spend, not save, and 40% say neither spending nor saving was particularly encouraged. A different picture emerges from the homes of people who went on to complete university degrees. Seventy-one percent were encouraged to save by their family. The rest were either taught to be extravagant or not encouraged in any particular attitude towards money.

THE BENEFITS OF SPORT

The more formal education you have, the more likely you are to think the main reason children should take part in sports and generally stay physically active is to improve their health and sense of well-being. The less formal education you have, the more likely you are to say the biggest reason for taking part in sports is to learn self-discipline.

Canadians with only a high school education are twice as likely as university grads to say they don't enjoy spending time with people who challenge their way of looking at the world. One in five high school grads express this feeling, compared to just one in ten university grads.

WHO DO WE WANT TO LIVE HERE?

Finishing high school seems to be almost a prerequisite for having a positive attitude towards immigrants. Half of those who did not complete high school want Canada to reduce its immigration levels, and think that we should welcome fewer immigrants than other developed countries. A quarter of those with some post-secondary education share this opinion, while only 14% of university graduates do—most say Canada's immigration levels should match those of similar-sized developed countries, or even outpace them. Thirty percent of people with higher education believe Canada should be recruit more immigrants than rival countries do.

It's also difficult to ignore the link between how long someone spent in school and how likely they are to express views a politician would be hesitant to voice. For example, 70% of university graduates believe a recent immigrant should have as much say in Canada's future as someone whose family has lived here for generations. Four out of every ten Canadians with some post-secondary education but no degree think this doesn't sound right. And half the people who didn't complete high school think it's nonsense.

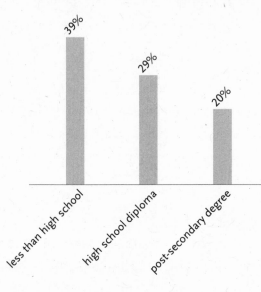

"I think Canada should let in more white immigrants but fewer visible minorities."

39% — less than high school
29% — high school diploma
20% — post-secondary degree

MONEY FOR THIS ART

People without a high school education don't believe tax money should go towards making films that are contrary to the public interest—meaning films that some consider distasteful or offensive. Only 39% think the government is wrong to withhold tax credits from these sorts of productions. Among high school graduates, 55% disapprove of a policy that would deny tax credits to these kinds of movies.

Two-thirds of university graduates say they'd like their local government to put more money into the arts. Fifty-three percent of high school dropouts say the same.

On the other hand, most university grads don't agree that governments are too short of money to support the arts. Most people with less education think governments simply can't afford to pay for artistic projects because other priorities need the money more.

FOREIGN AID FOR AIDS

People with a university education consider themselves well informed on the issue of HIV and AIDS, and 61% of them argue that Canada currently spends too little fighting the disease in foreign countries. (People with some post-secondary schooling are split evenly on this issue; 59% of those with high school diplomas feel that enough or too much is already being spent.) In fact, if you gathered together all the Canadians who believe too much money goes to combat AIDS overseas and asked to see their resumés, you'd find that only 6% hold a university degree.

CLIMATE CHANGE

People with more education worry about climate change. Sixty-five percent of university grads say they're extremely or definitely concerned, compared to half of the people with a high school diploma or less. This isn't because those of us who spend less time in school haven't heard the scientific explanations—high school grads are just as likely to respond that the main cause of climate change is the man-made gases trapped in the atmosphere. This group is simply less inclined to be alarmed about the situation; in fact, if you didn't go to university, you're twice as likely to agree that despair over global warming is the fault of pessimistic environmentalists and scientists trying to get attention. (Most university grads profoundly reject this claim.)

A weird wrinkle appears in this picture, however. It appears that, among those Canadians who haven't received higher education but who *do* accept the scientific explanations of global warming, the fear of climate change's impact is all the greater. Sixty-five percent of people who didn't pursue formal education after high school say that global warming is man-made, and the same proportion think that if we don't take drastic action right now, the human race might not last much longer than another couple of generations. The level of short-term concern is slightly lower among university grads—59% share this fear of imminent doom.

"I think the environment is the biggest issue facing our politicians today."

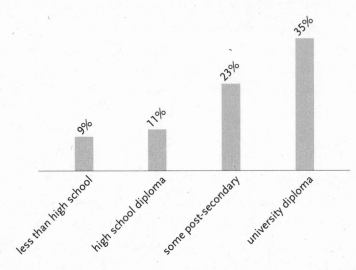

THOUGHTS ON DRUGS

People with a university education overwhelmingly support the setting up of safe injection sites in major cities—that is, facilities exempt from Canadian narcotics laws where addicts can go to inject themselves with drugs using clean needles provided for free. Seventy percent of university graduates approve of this kind of thing, compared to 54% of those with high school or college diplomas, and just 42% of Canadians who did not finish high school.

THE ROYAL QUESTION

People who stayed in school all the way through to university graduation experienced much less emotional hardship in 2005 when Prince Charles married Camilla Parker-Bowles. They were half as likely to disapprove of the marriage—only 17% were unhappy about it, compared to 27% of people with some post-secondary education or with a high school diploma. At the time, roughly a fifth of university graduates told our pollsters they didn't care about this royal affair.

Canadians with less formal education are more likely to care whether Camilla should take the title of Queen when Prince Charles becomes King (the vast majority believe she should decline the title and call herself something less regal; precise terms were not specified). Most Canadians who did not go to university want Prince Charles to skip his place in line for the throne and pass the crown straight to Prince William. University graduates are fairly evenly split on this question (and in any case, most of them want Canada to end its formal ties to the British monarchy).

VALEDICTION

Canadian grownups may want to see young people stay in school and add those impressive letters after their names, but while the kids pick up more education, they may also pick up some very different beliefs. We can't always be sure that more school leads *directly* to, say, weaker religious beliefs or greater concern about what environmental scientists are saying.

What we do know is that, regardless of education, there are marked differences between Canadians depending on how long they've been around, which leads us to the next chapter.

13 / The Young and the Old

H ere's where we sketch out how younger and older Canadians see the world differently. There's no opinion held by a teenager that's so inherently youthful that it couldn't also live in the mind of a retiree, and likewise no insight gained from experience so profound that it could not possibly be appreciated by a young adult. Nevertheless, years of experience growing older in this country, of seeing governments come and go, of seeing how a community changes over time, or how a an idea that seemed sound turned out to be a mistake . . . it all affects a person. When we group all the more experienced (or, to be blunt, older) Canadians, we notice trends in their opinions, tastes, and habits.

After we've surveyed adults, we split them up into groups called cohorts. The youngest cohort is 18 to 34. The intermediate cohort is 35 to 54. The well-seasoned, well-established, fully ripened senior cohort is made up of those aged 55 . . . and beyond. For brevity's sake, we'll forgo the euphemisms and call these cohorts younger, middle-aged, and ancient. No, scratch that. We'll call the last one older.

Older Canadians: A Thumbnail Sketch

They spend 6 minutes and 20 seconds in the shower, and appear nonplussed at the mention of eco-friendly clothing. They think the party with the best economic policies is either the Liberals or the Conservatives. If a fellow Canadian gets stuck on death row somewhere after a fair trial, good riddance. Regardless of what you think about seal hunting, the law is the law and illegal disruptions must be stopped. Chinese imports don't make safe playthings for grandchildren. Older Canadians didn't have savings accounts until they were about fifteen years old. They never get drunk and stranded, and rarely skip breakfast.

When Victoria Day weekend rolls around, half of the over-55s spend the time at home relaxing. Even though older Canadians don't usually spend the day actively remembering things about Queen Victoria, they know who she was and understand that this is supposedly a day in her honour. A third of older Canadians still think this is important.

"Victoria Day is a time to honour the reign of Queen Victoria and has historical meaning. It isn't simply a day off."

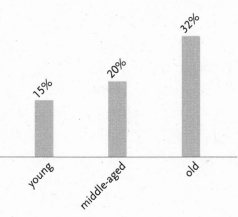

UNPREPARED FOR LIFE

When it comes to preparing for the autumn years, many Canadian seniors pay more attention to their deaths than to their lives. Nine in ten Canadians over the age of 65 have written a will. Half of them even have a cemetery plot picked out, and almost as many have called up an undertaker or taken other steps to prearrange their own funeral. But they haven't yet got around to calling a family member to discuss possible changes in living arrangements as they age.

Canadians aged 65 to 85 not currently receiving home health care

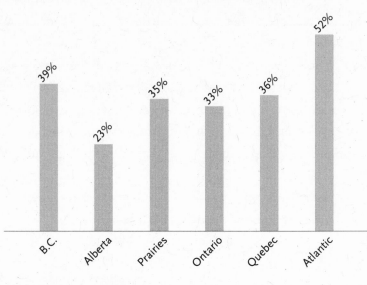

PREPARED FOR RETIREMENT

Before the home care decisions become abruptly important, the biggest question people ask about aging is probably, "Do we have enough money to retire?" This is the critical issue that will influence when they will stop working, more important than age or any of the other common concerns that may arise.

GET RICH QUICK

A big lottery win affects young and old workers differently. If they won $5 million tomorrow, most twenty-somethings would start a company or a new career, or possibly go back to school. A person over the age of 45 is likely to say they'd quit their job and retire. At some point during their thirties and forties, most Canadians apparently lose the urge to make a big splash or a dramatic change.

Whether still in the workforce or already retired, most Canadians express optimism about their retirement, saying they believe it will at least be a comfortable life. Only one out of every twenty feels strongly that retirement will not be financially comfortable. Half of the people surveyed expect some of their retirement savings to go towards health care costs. On average, Canadian retirees think they need a stash of $450,000 for a secure retirement, while those still working plan to save $895,709 before they take the plunge.

Most people expect their employer's pension to provide them with their largest source of income upon retiring. One-fifth of Canadians expect to rely on the government pension. One percent of Canadians believe that RRSPs will provide their best single source of income during retirement.

Before and after:

Is retirement a better life?

79%

56%

approaching retirement and expecting quality of life to improve

retired and quality of life has improved

BOOMERS, TAKE HEART

We directed stacks of questions at people between 50 and 69 years old, asking what retirement meant for them, which aspects of it seem exciting, which parts terrifying, and so on. One detail that jumped out straightaway was the difference between current retirees and the people who will retire in the next few years. It seems retirement may offer some people a pleasant surprise. We asked people approaching retirement if they expected their quality of life to improve, and compared that to the testimony of people who had recently retired.

One retirement perk is freedom from the alarm clock. Two-thirds of retired Canadians say they've banished it and no longer suffer that morning jolt of being woken up by a buzz, beep, ring, or radio. That doesn't mean retirement necessarily slows life down. Two-thirds of respondents say they continue to live life at the same pace as before they retired. Almost all of the Boomers we interviewed told us they are becoming more aware of the need for wellness and personal care. Two-thirds of the retired Boomers spend more time looking after themselves than they used to, although this change begins for many people before retirement—59% of the Boomers who haven't yet retired also said they've started to take better care of themselves.

STILL WORKING

As we work our way backwards into late middle age, older workers often agree that they live to work—they enjoy working and it's not just a necessary evil that must be done in order to pay the bills. Younger people tend to disagree.

This doesn't prevent many of those same older Canadians from agreeing with the statement, "I work to live; I need the paycheque but prefer to leave work at work." But one-quarter of the over-

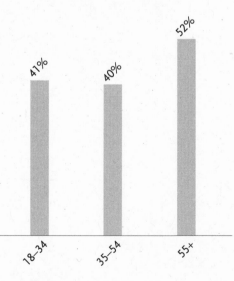

"I live to work—I enjoy it and it's not just to pay the bills."

18-34: 41%
35-54: 40%
55+: 52%

55s disagree with this, more than the roughly 17% of Canadians under 55 years old who disagree.

TIME FOR BOOKS

While more younger people than older people read a book last year, it's a fact that *more books* were read by people over 55. That's because those older people who do read read a lot.

Average number of books read in 2007 by people who did read a book

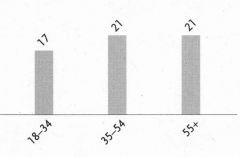

Science fiction and fantasy books find more fans among middle-aged readers (18%) than younger ones (13%). School-related textbooks, unsurprisingly, show up most often in younger people's booklists. No age group significantly leads another in mentioning religious texts among the books they've read recently. A fifth of the older readers listed history books (which showed up on only 4% of the younger and middle-aged readers' lists). A grand total of 2% of Canadian book readers read a book of poetry last year, which is slightly less than the percentage of Canadians overall who believe that Elvis Presley is still alive.

Now, because these poll results offer accuracy within only about 3 percentage points up or down, it is possible that a greater proportion of Canadian book readers spend their time reading poetry than

Canadians overall think Elvis still lives. (In case you're wondering, it is impossible that minus 1% of Canadians read poetry.) To properly compare apples with apples, however, we ought to count the poetry readers against the *total* adult population of Canada because the book readers themselves make up only 69%. This makes the chance very slim that poetry readers outnumber Elvis-believers nationwide. For what it's worth, both of these constituencies shrink in comparison to the number of people who think aliens visit our planet on a regular basis. At 20%, this opinion—strongly held or otherwise—usually outperforms support for the federal New Democratic Party. But we digress . . .

Elvis vs Poetry

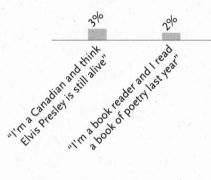

3% 2%

"I'm a Canadian and think Elvis Presley is still alive" "I'm a book reader and I read a book of poetry last year"

WORRIES

Older people fear identity theft more than the young do. In fact, twice as many older Canadians say they're very worried about it. Younger people tend to be only somewhat bothered by the idea or not too concerned. Canadians over the age of 55 are also twice as likely to say they've heard a lot about identity theft but still aren't sure exactly what it means. In an average group of five Canadian seniors, two would identify with this problem. In an average group of five young Canadian adults, just one would do so.

In Vancouver, older people express more fear of gang violence. Three-quarters of those over 45 say gang violence is a very serious problem that has increased a lot in the last few years. Only half of the younger residents feel this way. Most over-45s (60%) fear for the safety of family members and close friends due to the rise in gang violence. Younger adults (again, about 60%) aren't worried. Older Vancouver residents are twice as likely to say they've changed their behaviour due to their fears, avoiding downtown areas, not travelling alone on public transit during the late evenings, or generally reducing visits to restaurants and bars late at night.

TRADITIONS

Even though they're willing to ditch Canada's traditional policy of coming to the rescue of condemned criminals abroad, older people sometimes support an older way of doing things against the views of the younger generation. When debate sprang up in 2008 regarding whether the Peace Tower flag on Parliament Hill should be lowered every time a Canadian soldier is killed, younger Canadians overwhelmingly called for the flag lowering. Many in the older generations—four in ten—wanted to stick to the tradition of lowering the flag only on Remembrance Day, most likely because, to them, lowering the flag to half-mast for the military is an inclusive act that involves recognition of all who have fallen in current and previous conflicts, not just the deaths that might happen on any given unfortunate day. To them, the act speaks to the ages, not to the moment.

Nostalgia is wasted on the old. It's apparently more common for younger Canadian adults to feel attached to the one-cent coin. Fewer people under the age of 35 support the idea of abolishing it.

SQUINT AND SHOW YOUR TEETH

Very few people over the age of 55 consider eyeglasses to be sexy. Strangely enough, many young people find them a turn-on.* Most twenty-somethings say they'd rather lose 10 years of their life than go blind; a slight majority of older Canadians would not take this bargain. When asked about the physical qualities they most notice in other people, most 18-to-34-year-olds said it was the eyes. People over the age of 55 more commonly said it was the smile. Ninety-two percent of over-55s own and wear prescription eyeglasses but they're much less likely than younger people to wear contact lenses.

"I own and wear contact lenses."

28%
4%
18-34
55+

In British Columbia, nearly half of the older people we spoke with think it's impolite to wear sunglasses when having a conversation. Only a quarter of the province's young folks share this view. (If you're a woman who really wants to commit a faux pas with a typical older person in British Columbia, try doing the above at the beach while sunbathing topless, wearing a thong, and drinking alcohol with your picnic. All of these activities get the thumbs-up from the majority of young adults but a thumbs-down from the older generation.)

Editor's note: The eyeglasses, not the old people.

INTERMISSION: MIDDLE AGE

Generally, Canadians in mid-life answer opinion polls in such a way that their age group lands precisely in the middle of the road, with the old on one side and the young on the other. On a couple of issues, however, middle-aged Canadians do stick their necks out, so we'll pause briefly to consider these moments.

JUNK OR TREASURE?

Open up the average newspaper and a handful—sometimes a bucketful—of advertising flyers fall to the ground. Companies pay to piggyback on the delivery system that newspapers use. A majority of Canadians say they enjoy reading these inserts, and this feeling is strongest among middle-aged and older people, 70% of whom like the ads. Among younger people the majority is thinner—just 55% enjoy them, and in fact the number of young Canadians who really *hate* flyers roughly equals the number of older Canadians who absolutely love them (in each case, it's about 15%). Two-thirds of older Canadians prefer to look through the ads in a newspaper than watch commercials on TV, and even more say they always look through the papers for information on the best sales during holiday weekends. But it's wrong to think of these activities as typical only of the hawk-eyed retiree with a pair

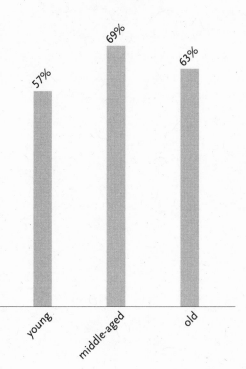

"I keep inserts and flyers for days to reread them."

57% young
69% middle-aged
63% old

of scissors ready for clipping out coupons. If one age group shows a particular weakness for marketing leaflets and newspaper ads, it's actually the middle-aged.

A quarter of Canada's middle-aged people would undergo plastic surgery if they could afford it. The idea is less appealing to the over-55s, less than a fifth of whom would be interested in any cosmetic surgery.

CONCERNED CITIZENS

Middle-aged people often take the lead in community battles. A quarter of middle-aged Canadians say they're really angry about the level of crime in their neighbourhood and are either doing something about it already or are going to act soon "for sure." Just a fifth of older people, and a sixth of younger adults, express themselves this way.

The middle-aged are the most likely to want a referendum on the Senate, the most concerned about food safety, the most keen to pay for more food inspectors, and the most solid supporters of Canada taking part in military combat overseas.

Among those aged 40 to 60, two-thirds admit to suffering from memory lapses frequently in recent years.

YOUNGER CANADIANS

Eight minutes is too short for a good shower. Young Canadian adults need, on average, nine minutes and 40 seconds to get clean. If you're a typical young Canadian, you might find the other sorts of questions we ask to be tiring and difficult.

While they're happy to respond to questions of principle, when faced with a purely political query, younger adults as a group go quiet on us. For instance, during the buildup to one recent provincial election in Alberta, young adults there pointed to "Don't know" when asked which party was best able to deal with health care issues, education, housing affordability issues, and oil royalties, as well as the party with the best approach to tackling crime and handling the economy. At least they were consistent. If some canny politicians founded a real-life Don't Know Party and managed to get this option placed on the ballot sheet, it might really stir up the political landscape.

Seventy percent of younger Canadians say they're more likely to buy an article of clothing that claims to be eco-friendly; 60% aren't bothered by "made in China" labels on their children's toys.

Apparently, however, younger adults do tune in to the occasional political debate, since they're able to express slightly more respect for the debating skills of elected politicians than older people do. Among Canadians under the age of 35, four out of every ten describe the quality of political discussion in this country as good. For those over the age of 35, the verdict is harsher, with seven out of ten calling the debates poor or terrible. On second thought, maybe that vote of confidence from younger people is because they usually aren't paying attention. The image flips when people rate religious groups' contribution to the public debate. Then, 41% of over-55s call the debate good, while 70% of younger Canadians say it's poor or terrible.

POLITICAL WATERS

Thirty percent of older Canadians feel very confident that Canada has enough fresh water for the long-term; 19% of younger adults voice such confidence. Most young adults strongly believe it's wrong to commodify water—that is, to buy and sell the rights to withdraw it from a source and use it. Older Canadians are inclined to agree, but only a minority of them express strong feelings about the matter.

Younger people take strong stances on the issues, despite their apparent disregard for formal political parties. They advocate seeking clemency for death-row Canadians overseas as well as for death-row seals on the Atlantic coast, whatever the pesky laws may be about disrupting hunters' livelihoods.

Continuing on the legal front, younger people express stronger opinions about the need for fair access to the legal system. In British Columbia, for instance, 70% of the young speak strongly in favour of legal aid services, compared to just over half of the older people who feel those are important. Many older adults don't much want to pick up the tab for the lawyers helping immigrants and refugee claimants. Young people support this with near unanimity.

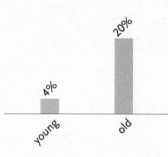

"I don't think it's important to provide legal aid for immigration/refugee hearings."

It's hard enough to keep abreast of current politics, let alone the politicians who ruled two centuries ago. Queen Victoria throws a few young Canadians for a loop. One in ten can't say where she ruled, and one in twenty (not wanting to be caught out by a trick question) confidently told us that she's not a real queen! Young adults don't waste the Victoria Day long weekend doing nothing at home, remembering a possibly fictional monarch. They head off to a bar, a cottage, or somewhere natural and outdoorsy.

RESPONSIBLE DRINKERS?

Adults under the age of 35 do know some things. They're familiar with the experience of realizing you've had too much to drink and discovering that your planned method of getting home isn't going to work. This predicament prompts the need for some quick thinking on the spot, which is difficult to do while intoxicated.

When older people go out and drink without having made a plan to get home safely, it's usually because they're not planning to drink very much. It's rarely in the carefree spirit of trusting that a safe option will just show up when it's needed—only 7% say this is their typical attitude. But many younger people are comfortable with improvising. Thirty percent of the young Canadians who generally go out drinking without a plan for the end of the night say it's because they trust they'll find a safe way to get home (or wherever else they end up).

RESPONSIBLE SAVERS

Today's twenty-somethings are 3.5 times more likely to have grown up in a household where spending was encouraged (14%) than Canadians over 65 (4%). This makes sense intuitively because we know that older Canadians experienced the Great Depression, which made them frugal and ensured that they instilled frugality in their children as well. Many of us who are now middle-aged recall our parents telling how they paid cash for cars and got rid of their mortgage as fast as they could. So a common stereotype is one of an older generation of people who opened early savings accounts, socking money away while today's youthful spendthrifts were out spending, not giving any thought to savings until well into their later years.

Like most stereotypes, it is not completely true. In fact, Canadians who are 18 to 30 today opened their first savings account when they were 10 years old (the average is 10 years, 5 months). Those who are over 65 today opened their first savings account at age 15 (average: 15 years, 7 months).

Furthermore, 44% of Canadians 18 to 30 today had those savings accounts before they were 10 years old, compared to just 19% of those who are over 65 today. The apparent reason for this is that many older Canadians weren't raised with any kind of instruction in financial management. Thirty-seven percent of people this age say that in their youth they were not encouraged to spend or to save. Twenty-four percent of younger people today report this lack of encouragement in either direction.

It is interesting to note that the goal in opening a savings account has changed significantly over the generations. Fifty-three percent of those over 65 indicate that they save money "for a rainy day," versus 36% of those who are 18 to 30. Only 21% of Canadians over 65 say their savings accounts were established for specific financial goals, compared to 36% of those aged 18 to 30.

GENEROUS YOUTH

Teenagers say that out of every $100 they spend, they give $5 to charities involved in development efforts outside Canada. As a percentage, this level of giving is more than double the federal government's foreign aid budget, which hovers around 2%. On the whole, teenagers tell pollsters they feel they could comfortably increase their gifts to global charities to $7 out $100. Ontario youth feel they ought to aim for nearly $8. However, Canadians teens believe that other issues are even more pressing; 40% think protecting the global ecosystem counts as the world's most serious problem.

RESPONSIBLE BREAKFASTS

Young people aren't big fans of breakfast. They skip it regularly. They like to snack, though. If you could observe all Canadian adults on a set of huge video screens at any given moment, you'd see twice as many younger people eating a granola bar and four times as many drinking a glass of chocolate milk as you would see older people doing so. Actually, some of them might be drinking the milk straight from the carton. (We did not ask people to specify.)

"My favourite meal is breakfast."

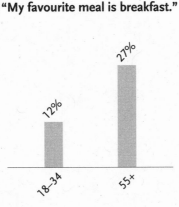

ENERGY CONSERVATION

Roughly half of Canadian adults under the age of 35 own a home. Among those who do, many think energy-efficient appliances play the most important role in conserving energy in the home. Those over 35 (most of whom are property owners) focus on appliances less; they're more likely to put their faith in good insulation. The vast majority (86%) of these older people claim to have done something or a lot to make their homes more energy efficient. A third of the young admit they've done little or nothing in this regard. Most older people have insulated their homes and sealed air leaks, allowing them to turn down their heat in winter. However, the younger generation can claim the lead in other greenhouse gas–fighting measures such as taking public transit or turning down the air conditioning in the summer.

STAND UP STRAIGHT AND DYE IT

The younger a person is, the more likely he or she is to want a tall romantic partner. The older a person is, the more likely he or she is to be attracted to sandy-coloured hair.

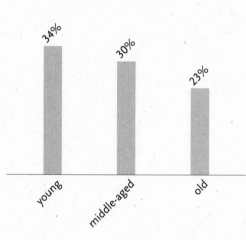

"My ideal romantic partner is tall."

As far as sexual partners go, most people over 55 prefer a warm lover to a scorching-hot one. (Hopefully when we asked this question people didn't think we we talking about body temperature. A literally scorching-hot lover might struggle to find *anyone* to share a bed with.) It's interesting to see that there is no difference between younger and middle-aged Canadians in this regard. An equal portion—about

40%—of people in those cohorts say their ideal mate would be a scorcher. Thirteen percent of older people would want this.

"My ideal romantic partner has sandy hair."

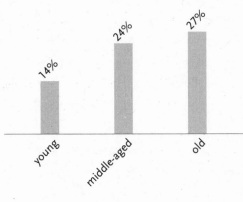

FINAL WORDS

What makes people grow old? Well, one answer is obvious: Time makes us old. But that's not the only reason for grey hair and high blood pressure. One of the great divides between young idealists and gritty realists seems to be the experience of having kids. If we want to know what somebody's thinking, we don't just ask how old they are, we ask if they share their household with children. So that's the next stop on our tour of the Canadian psyche.

14 / THE PARENT

Kids can change your mind. Well, first they change your hormones, *then* they work away at your mind—they're smart that way. Pregnant women gain weight, feel sick, eat funny things, need more back rubs, forget how to fall asleep, and all of this understandably lends a different hue to the world around them. A man in a close relationship with a pregnant woman won't escape hormonal change either—just ask your average male marmoset, who gains an extra fifth of his body weight while his partner is pregnant.* Or, if you're not on speaking terms with any marmosets, ask an average Canadian father-to-be, whose body gets heavier and kicks up production of a substance called prolactin, a useful chemical that is somewhat wasted on men since its main role is to stimulate the production of breast milk. Still, as they say, it's the thought that counts.

TESTING FOR PARENTHOOD

The fact is, parents who currently have kids living at home answer some questions differently from people with no kids. Have a look at the test on the following page and see for yourself.

---

*And that's just the beginning. Marmoset dads can look forward to growing dense mounds of dendritic spines and vasopressin V1a receptors in the top front part of the brain, just behind the forehead. Scientists have yet to figure out whether these new mounds are responsible for causing male monkeys to think up corny jokes and perform other embarrassing "dad behaviours."

THE IPSOS TEST FOR PARENTHOOD

Below are ten statements that can be used to identify people who have kids living at home.

Statement	More likely to live with kids	Less likely to live with kids
Our favourite vegetable is either corn, peas, carrots, or broccoli.	•	
Every month, we put some money into a savings account.		•
I'm extremely upset about the Chinese behaviour in Tibet.		•
Sometimes I read the newspaper just for the ads and flyers. I don't bother reading the stories.	•	
When I buy a toy for a child, I always scrutinize it extremely carefully to make sure it's safe.		•
I eat vegetables every day.		•
I hope I have a wealthy relative somewhere whom I don't know about yet.	•	
Flu season worries me.	•	
I find freshly poured cement tempting to touch.	•	

THE VEGGIE DIVIDE

People who don't have kids are twice as likely as people with children to say mushrooms are their household's favourite vegetable. They're three and a half times as likely to say it's asparagus. If you go into a child-free home and ask to see the favourite vegetable, most of the time (64%) you won't be presented with broccoli, corn, carrots, or peas. However, if you go into a home and see a kid running down the stairs, the chances shoot up that you'll be told the household's favourite vegetable is one of those four, with corn out in front.

"In our house, corn is one of the top three vegetables."

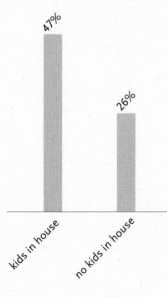

The king vegetable is still the potato, kids or no kids. Zucchini is hardly anybody's favourite. Most adults who live with children do not eat vegetables every day, and a quarter of parents blame their children for this.

MONEY TO SAVE

Most people with kids say there's no money left for savings after they've paid the bills. Only a quarter of them even have a savings account. People without kids can usually save some money, and they're much more likely to have a special bank account just for savings. Parents often say they don't have enough time to think about or plan for their goals (23% admit to this).

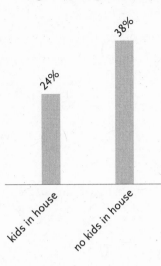

"I've got a savings account."

24%
kids in house

38%
no kids in house

JUST FOR THE ADS

People with kids read more advertising flyers. Three-quarters enjoy the page ads and service inserts that come with a newspaper. Only two-thirds of people without kids feel the same way. Three-quarters of those with kids go through the ads in the paper looking for information on sales. Only two-thirds of those without kids do this. People with kids keep the flyers around for days.

TOY SAFETY

Strangely enough, it's the Canadians who *don't* have kids at home who are slightly more likely to pay really, really close scrutiny to the safety of toys they buy for children—44% compared to 39% of parents. Among the people with kids, the most popular answer on this issue is that they're being careful but not changing their buying behaviour a great deal. Parents of young children are no more likely than the rest of the population to express concern about the safety of toys being imported into Canada. (The tendency of older people to worry more about imports might explain this fact.)

In the buildup to Christmas and other wintertime cultural celebrations, eight in ten people with kids at home buy toys for children. Just over half of people without kids also buy toys. Once the toys are in the house, played with, and strewn all over the carpet, one out of every five Canadian parents never clean them. Two in five scrub them with soap and water, one rinses them with water, and the other one sprays them with antibacterial solution.

FAMILY HISTORY

People get interested in their family histories for all sorts of reasons, and there's nothing in our polls to suggest that living with children drives people to start looking up their family tree. We do notice, however, that a quarter of the people who *don't* have kids at home say that the death of a family member would be the main reason they'd take an interest in their ancestors. Parents are half as likely to give the death of a relative as the most likely reason for their curiosity about their family, but slightly *more* inclined to hope they have a very wealthy relative somewhere that they don't know about. The possibility of an unknown wealthy relative appeals to 46% of people with children and to 38% of those without.

FLU TEST

According to our surveys, a parent's first response when her, she, or someone in the house gets the flu is to stay in bed, take a pill, and drink juice. Only 7% will immediately make an appointment to see a doctor. Roughly the same number say they've never had the flu.

People with kids under 17 at home are more apt to worried about flu season—37% say they're worried, compared to just 23% of people without small children. This probably makes sense, given that 17% of adults who live with small kids get the virus in any given year. Only 10% of those without kids get the flu. Twenty percent of adults between 18 and 34 are likely to get it. People without kids at home are twice as likely to visit a doctor when they get the flu. This number includes all the older people whose children have grown up.

"When I got the flu this year, I went to see the doctor."

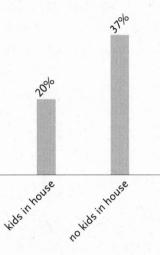

kids in house — 20%

no kids in house — 37%

SICK KIDS

Here's what children in British Columbia told us about their health:

- 42% of those aged 15 and 16 said they'd taken prescription medication that year.
- 80% of girls and 70% of boys stayed home from school at some point because they were sick.
- 44% visited a doctor to find out what was wrong with them.
- 10% reported a serious health problem.
- 5% suffered a serious injury.
- 2% stayed overnight in a hospital.
- 1% thought the hardest thing about achieving good health was the challenge of not watching so much television.

THE WET CEMENT TEST

This is a real long shot as a test for parenthood. But we found out that quite a few parents—more than a third—say they'd be tempted to touch a patch of freshly poured cement on a sidewalk if no one was looking. Less than a quarter of non-parents make this admission. That doesn't mean that having kids makes people behave badly in every respect. For instance, people without kids are more likely than parents to admit they'd have a hard time resisting touching the hat of a Buckingham Palace guard if it passed within groping distance.

Parenthood doesn't seem to affect broader moral issues. Having kids at home seems to have no overall impact on whether Canadians think a court should intervene when a parent's religious beliefs rule out a blood transfusion for a child.

MOST PARENTS SAY . . .

Sometimes, instead of comparing parents to everyone else, we ask special questions just for people with kids. In answering these questions, parents give us small and large details about how they hope their children's lives will unfold.

The following statements turn out to be true for the majority of today's Canadian parents:

- "My kids get at least nine hours sleep per night, but I don't."
- "My kids exercise four times a week."
- "My children spend less than two hours watching TV. (I limit their television-watching.)"
- "My children eat breakfast every day."
- "My children can walk to a playground or a park in less than ten minutes."
- "I never smoke."
- "My children don't ever drink alcohol or smoke."
- "I drink beer and wine occasionally."

- "We have at least one family meal together every day."
- "I take part in a physical recreation activity with my kids at least once a week."

Some of these statements outpoll the others. The most popular is actually the smoking one—96% of parents say their kids never smoke. This figure is high partly because it includes the parents of very young children, but even among the parents of teenagers, 85% believe that their kids never touch cigarettes. (The Canadian Lung Association estimates that one in five teens smoke at least occasionally.) A less popular statement is the one about recreation. While most parents join their kids in playing soccer, hockey, or some other activity that requires physical exercise, a large minority (37%) say they don't often do this. In families with yearly incomes of under $35,000, only half play sports with their kids.

Ninety-three percent of Canadian parents believe that they are primarily responsible for the health of their kids. Kids are evenly divided on whether parents or children shoulder the most responsibility.

"I'm a parent, and I'd give money to help poor kids participate in sports."

67%

33%

yes

no

THE COST OF SPORT

Most parents are able to pay for their kids to take part in any organized sport they want, and most say they've got enough money leftover to help out low-income families so that their kids can take part in sports too.

If you think the parents who said they wouldn't give money seem ungenerous, it's worth noting that the same proportion of parents admit that they've had to hold their own kids back from participating in team sports because of the cost. In fact, this is as issue for most parents whose household income is under $60,000. More moms (48%) than dads (26%) say their kids have missed out on organized sport.

PARENTAL AMBITIONS

Parents of young children often want their kids to grow up to be scientists. The older the parents, the more likely they are to say this.

"I have a kid aged 2 to 5, and I want him/her to be a scientist."

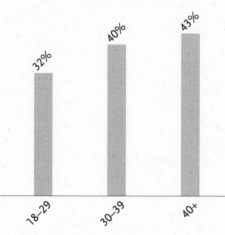

The main reason for the difference in response rates here is that younger parents are the most likely to want their child to be "anything he/she wants to be"—one-quarter of parents under 30 give this response. (And so do a quarter of moms, whatever their age. Dads are the ones most likely to say they're hoping to raise a scientist.) Parents of girls are the most inclined to raise a scientist. As far as science careers go, four times as many young girls have parents who want them to become veterinarians; parents who want boys to be scientists usually choose "engineer, doctor, or dentist."

Less than 1% of Canadian parents hope their child will grow up to be a writer. Even fewer are hoping to raise farmers. And out of 1,000 parents consulted for this survey, just one wanted their child to grow up to be a baker.

It's more common to hope your young child becomes an astronaut than to want him or her to be an accountant.

Parents say today's kids must be better prepared to enter the work-force than children in the past used to be because these days they're expected to compete for jobs against workers in other countries, not just against other Canadians. Since university fees are unaffordable for many students, scholarships today are more desirable than ever. Nine out of ten mothers say their child needs to excel in school in order to get a scholarship for post-secondary education so as to have a chance to reach the top of the global heap.

Nine out of ten mothers believe that their kid is either average or above average compared to their classmates. Fathers are even more confident—most say their kid's grades are above average. But kids don't win scholarships with grades that are merely above average, so four out of every ten parents who describe their child's performance as such take the extra step of getting a tutor or giving their child some sort of extra schooling. Twenty percent of parents say their above-average student gets modified instruction in the classroom;15% have arranged for "enrichment" outside of school. Ten percent have enrolled their child in special groups or activities in school. Two per-cent have let their child skip a grade. One percent enrolled their child in an immersion program.

Among the few parents who admit their child's grades are below average, most are taking action—60% say the child gets extra help to improve their grades. This strategy is not evenly spread across the country, however. Seventy percent of Ontario and Prairie parents have arranged special help for kids who are under-performing, compared to 41% of parents in the Atlantic provinces.

Most parents feel that the school system is too inflexible to deal with the different ways that children learn. More women (62%) feel this way than men (49%). The vast majority of parents agree that their child needs some help in reaching his or her potential. Only a quarter of parents think their kid will do just fine if left to his or her own devices.

WHAT'S MORE IMPORTANT?

A Canadian parent is more likely to want schoolteachers to educate their kids about farms than to talk about healthy food choices.

Seventy percent of parents of elementary school–aged kids support putting farm-related lessons into the curriculum. This feeling is even stronger among parents of high school students. These parents want their kids to learn about the effect of farming on the environment and about what farmers do to protect nature.

Only half of the parents we talked to want healthy eating to be part of the school curriculum.

BUT FIRST THINGS FIRST: BREAKFAST

Every aspiring astronaut needs a hearty meal to start the day. But when it comes to deciding what to put on the table, Canadian parents make different decisions, depending on what part of the country they live in. British Columbia parents are the most likely to give their children milk to drink. Two-thirds say this is the typical breakfast drink for their kids. Half of Ontario parents say the same. If you're a kid in Ontario, it's very common to drink juice with breakfast—a third of Ontario kids start the day this way, compared to just a fifth of the British Columbians.

Juice beats milk as a lunchtime drink. But by dinnertime, milk is back on top. Only one in ten Prairie kids usually drink pop at dinnertime. Not very many British Columbia kids are allowed to do this either. However, when families eat out at a restaurant or order takeout, pop jumps into first place, way ahead of milk and juice. Six out of ten west-coast kids order soft drinks when they're dining out.

PEANUT BUTTER OR GRILLED CHEESE?

The most popular sandwich among Canadian children is grilled cheese. Peanut butter and jelly comes in a distant second, while third place is shared by tuna and bologna sandwiches. (That's tuna or bologna, not both at the same time.) Two out of five parents say their kids like grilled cheese the best, making it twice as popular as the runner-up.

JUST FOR GIRLS

We did a survey just for the mothers of daughters. Specifically, we wanted to find out how preteen girls cope with the stresses of social life. Our survey focused on that fraught occasion, the sleepover. Here's what we discovered.

Most girls enjoy sleepover parties with friends. Their mothers know this, and understand that these parties can affect their daughters' self-esteem. It's very common for moms to get involved in planning sleepover parties for preteen girls—80% of moms agree that it's sometimes necessary to help work out the guest list in order to avoid hurting any classmates. Who gets the nod and who doesn't is the main source of social anxiety related to sleepovers—40% of mothers say their own daughter has felt left out at some point because she did not get invited to a party. Once the guest list is settled, an even higher number of moms think it's important to confer with the mothers of party attendees.

Once the party has started, however, most moms stay out of the way in order to let girls be girls. It's a rare parent (about one in seven) who thinks it's better to take a prominent role in the party. And for three out of four girls, these parties are problem-free.

So what's that other girl's problem? Well, it's not unusual for some of the girls to come home from sleepover parties a bit upset and more self-conscious about their body image. One in five mothers have noticed this effect. Almost all moms claim to find it easy to talk with preteen daughters about what happens at sleepover parties, and these are the activities they hear about:

"My preteen girl takes part in these sleepover activities at parties."

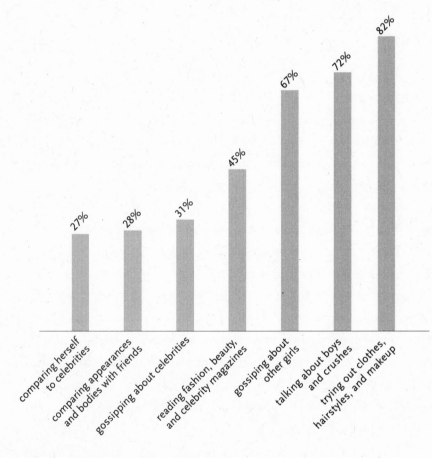

It's easy to imagine how these activities could cause preteens to feel the heightened emotions described by some mothers. In conclusion: the typical Canadian mom of the typical Canadian preteen girl does not worry much about how sleepover parties affect her daughter's self-image. But that's little comfort to the many girls who aren't in the majority at these parties.

MOM VERSUS DAD

Kids, including grown-up ones, put more thought into gifts for their mothers than presents for their fathers. Some Quebecers claim that they put an equal amount of care into the gifts for each parent, but even in this province, these offspring are in the minority.

"When buying gifts, I usually put more thought into . . ."

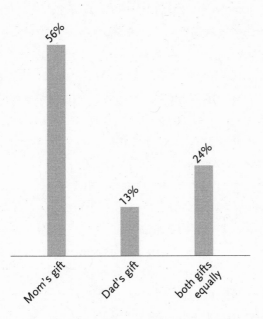

In fact, Father's Day often gets forgotten—or wilfully ignored. It is a more recent invention, after all, having started in North America just 100 years ago, compared to the sixteenth-century Christian practice of observing "Mothering Sunday." A quarter of Canadians say they've ignored Father's Day in the past.

> **Forty percent of mothers say the worst Mother's Day gift they ever received was "nothing at all."**

ADOPTION

Not all of the parents referred to in this chapter are biological ones who underwent those chemical changes we mentioned earlier. Some are legal guardians, and a few have adopted children. The latter two situations are actually less common than some might think. Out of every 20 Canadians, just one has seriously considered adopting a child, and two have considered the notion semi-seriously. You might need to gather 30 Canadians together to find one who's actually adopted a kid.

However, in that same group of 20, you'd probably find three people who would tell you someone in their family has put a child up for adoption (and one more who isn't sure if this has happened). More than half of the group—maybe 12 people—have a close friend or relative who was adopted. If you asked how many in the group had experienced adoption in some form, either as a parent or a child, two people would raise their hands.

When seeking opinions on adoption, we asked people a difficult question: How do you rate the media coverage of this issue? Many people, confronted with this question out of the blue, could not come up with an answer. If you were among the 18 people in the group of 20 above who had no experience of adoption, it's quite likely that you wouldn't notice what the media has to say one way or the other. So we were surprised that Quebecers seem to have been paying attention. Whereas a third of British Columbians and a quarter of Ontarians weren't sure how to rate the media coverage, the vast majority of

Quebecers asserted that the media coverage was favourable. Only 9% said they weren't sure how to rate it.

As a general issue, adoption wins approval from practically everybody, with most people agreeing that government leaders should give more attention to adoption issues, particularly the adoption of children who are currently in foster care. Canadians become more cautious when asked about the desirability of adopting Aboriginal children or children from other countries but still agree that more attention from government—whatever that attention might consist of—would be a good idea. Quebecers again stand out with stronger opinions in favour of giving more attention to finding adopters for Canadian kids.

It's very rare to believe that adopted children will not love their parents as much as they would have loved the people who first gave life to them, and also extremely unusual to think that parents get less satisfaction from raising an adopted child than from raising their own flesh and blood. The collective voice of Ontario, if we add up everybody's opinions on both sides of the issue, is that adopting a child is actually more satisfying than raising one's own offspring. (It's more common to express that view than to say the opposite.)

Out of the 1,556 Canadians we talked to, only 9 individuals told us they thought it was very unlikely that parents would love an adopted child as much one they gave birth to; 1,100 people figured parents very likely would love an adopted child equally, and a further 328 people said they agreed somewhat. Younger people are the only ones who seem inclined to think the biology issue is very important—10% of those aged 18 to 24 say either that parents are unlikely to love adopted kids as much, or that they're not sure one way or the other. Among people over the age of 35, 95% say the blood relationship has no impact on how much a parent will love the child.

So, Overall

Any parent will tell you that having children made a big difference in their life. This makes it even more surprising that so many opinion polls don't show big overall differences between today's parents and the rest of the population. The split on, say, how tempting some wet cement is doesn't stand out nearly as much as the differences across parts of the country or between generations. When we poll people with kids, we get the same responses as usual about the country's foreign policy and tax system and only slightly different responses on issues like the environment and crime (parents worry more about both, but only by a couple of percentage points). The bigger differences seem to relate to smaller things: the vegetables and grilled-cheese sandwiches people eat when kids are around, what happens to the flyers and coupons, and the likely temperature of what goes on behind closed doors.

"I want a scorching-hot lover in bed."

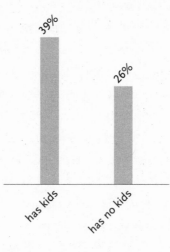

15 / The Wired Ones

The vast majority of Canadians own a computer with Internet access. Eight in ten young adults have one at home, and while older adults have generally been behind on the technology trends, they are catching up—seven in ten people over the age of 55 now have Internet at home. Almost as many own a cellphone.

At the time this book goes to press, it's still unusual to own a PDA, the hand-held gizmo that stores calendars, documents, etc., and connects wirelessly to the Internet so you can send e-mails while walking down the street, holding a second cellphone against one ear with your hunched shoulder and eating a muffin. One-quarter of people earning more than $80,000 a year own a PDA.

Twenty percent of people who earn less than $40,000 a year own neither a computer, a cellphone, a gaming console, a hand-held game system, nor a PDA. It's almost unheard of for someone who earns over $80,000 to own none of these, but a stubborn 1% of rich Luddites are still holding out. In the middle-income bracket, seventy-five percent of those who earn between $40,000 and $80,000 a year own a cellphone and 42% have a gaming console. Just 5% own none of the items on our list of digital gadgets below.

Gadget	Teenagers who own one (%)	Adults who own one (%)
digital music player	79	40
digital camera	41	75
cellphone	37	77
their own computer	33	94

TUNING IN TO THE LIVE STREAM

So much for the state of gadgets today. The whole idea of putting the latest facts about digital life into a printed book is old school (a writer on the online Urban Dictionary figures this term refers to the era of the very first computer generation, the people who owned personal computers running off Basic language without a hard drive and who played games like Pong; the point is, it's a generation after the Baby Boomers of 1945–65).

If we'd written this book back in mid-2007, we'd have noted that 60% of Canadians went shopping online, or at least browsed products using their computer. One year later, that number hit 70%. Meanwhile, the proportion of Canadians downloading television shows and movies rose from 20% to 25% during the same period. Almost everyone has been satisfied with their Internet experiences at any given stage, but the cable and phone companies have kept selling faster connections with the promise of better live streaming of movies, music, and so on, and most of us have kept buying them (even though only half of Canadians expressed any interest in watching TV on their computers). Between us sending this paragraph off to the printer and you turning to this page, the wired world has sped up again, and a whole new set of opinions have been posted on the Ipsos website.

So, instead of calling the information we have right at this moment "the latest facts," we'll grab the chance to become historians. You, the reader of the future (possibly only a few weeks into our future!), can see if your own techno-knowledge leaves us far behind in the dusty past.

WHAT WE ANCIENT CANADIANS USED TO THINK ABOUT DIGITAL TECHNOLOGY (IN 2008)

- Seventy-five percent of us thought Internet gambling was legal. It wasn't. Gambling on the Internet was against the law in Canada.
- Only 7% of us blogged.
- Fifty percent of people over 55 claimed to store files and important

documents online. Only 31% of young adults said they did this.

- Two percent of older Canadians said they'd had an e-mail address for more than 20 years; 8% had kept the same e-mail address for 15 years.
- Nearly 50% of young adults maintained at least three e-mail addresses.
- Only a smallish chunk of Canadians used their real name or their company name as their e-mail alias. Most used either a nickname, a variation of their name, a personality trait, or a fun or suggestive moniker.
- Seventy-five percent of Canadians strongly agreed that having an Internet service at home gives children an advantage in academic pursuits. The remaining quarter agreed somewhat with this statement.
- Only 6% of us hadn't noticed that children need home Internet access to complete school assignments. In Saskatchewan, 40% of residents said this was only somewhat true, a less emphatic view than that expressed in the rest of the country.
- Adults reported visiting a multitude of websites for a wide variety of reasons. Teens just visited social networking sites and places to download music and movies or play games. Sixty percent of teens visited online social networking sites almost daily, while 30% of adults had never been to one. Thirty-three percent of teens downloaded digital music several times a week. Very few adults did this as frequently.
- Thirty-three percent of Canadians posted their profile on a networking site or online social community. Ten percent visited these sites and decided not to post a profile on any of them.
- Forty percent of adults who went online regularly clicked on web ads.
- Fifty percent of the adults we spoke with listened to Internet radio stations.

TEENS ONLINE

So what's the most widespread reason for a Canadian teenager to go online? No, it's not to update their profile or even to go searching for X-rated pictures. It's to do research for schoolwork (at least, that's what they tell us). Online schoolwork is even more common than e-mail. When they're at school, older teens spend about seven hours a week doing online work.

This image of the teenager obediently researching the Battle of the Plains of Abraham doesn't allay parents' fears, however, and not just because half of the teenagers have noticed their friends using the Internet to cheat on school projects. The question of what else kids get up to online nags at just about every parent and guardian. By the time a Canadian child reaches the age of 13, they almost certainly have Internet access at home—in our survey, only one out of a hundred Canadian teens lacked this resource—and 40% of parents and guardians said they figured teens were probably visiting websites adults wouldn't approve of. Only 25% of parents and guardians feel certain their kids aren't accessing some sort of wicked or dangerous website. Twenty percent of parents admit they are unfamiliar with online chat rooms. Thirty percent don't know much about blogs. Fifty percent of the fathers we spoke with couldn't tell us what happens on popular social networking sites.

Parents share various tricks for dealing with their teens' online activities. Most snoop in the browser histories on their computers to retrace a teenager's web explorations and find out what content those sites offer. Moms are the most likely to do this—67% check the sites their teenagers are visiting (or at least, the sites the teens haven't somehow concealed). Thirty percent of parents post rules next to the computer for the child to follow, and almost all of the people we asked (92%) said they've spoken with their teens about the dangers of the Internet. These conversations don't always lead to firm rules, however—only 70% said they had instructed their teens about what counted as acceptable and unacceptable online activities.

Most of the parents and guardians under 35 (54%) said they've put parental controls on their Internet browsers to stop teens from going too far astray. Only a quarter of older Canadian parents use these control options. And funnily enough, parents with university degrees are the least likely to use software that limits their teens' web-browsing choices. Only 28% do this, compared to 40% of parents without a degree. Also, highly educated parents are less likely to go through their teens' browser histories—only 56% admitted to doing this, compared to almost 70% of other parents.

Half of Canada's parents claim to know their teens' online aliases. Seventy percent worry about teens encountering online scams. Sixty percent worry about cyber-bullying. And that's just the start—inappropriate language, swearing, pornography, sexual predators . . . most parents fear all of these evils.

TEEN VIEWS

One question we've yet to ask is how many teens worry about their parents snooping into their web-browser histories. If you're a teenager who's a bit alarmed to discover your mother has probably done this already, then maybe it's time to learn some techniques to cover your tracks. And if you're a parent who's alarmed to find out that your teen might be capable of hiding their activities, here's a comforting idea: Most teens aren't as tech-savvy as older people believe. A recent poll helped dispel the myth of the constantly wired Canadian teenager. Only a quarter of teens claim to be tech experts. A quarter say they're not very skilled at all. The rest describe their web knowledge as just fairly skilled, although perhaps they're being modest.

Among younger teens, almost all report that their parents exercise a significant influence on their online activities. This supervision ends around the middle of teenagehood; among older teens, fewer than 10% say their parents have any say in their online surfing expeditions. Aside from snooping through browser histories, the usual methods for controlling a kid's web browsing are to put the computer in an area where it can easily be observed and to write or announce guidelines about what's acceptable.

Most teenagers admit to being concerned about their security online. This is especially true of teenage girls, who are well aware of the horror stories. They usually remember being warned by their parents about the dangers of online predators.

Hooked to the Wire?

Way back in 2004, we found that teens spent about 13 hours a week online. When we checked in again four years later, that number hadn't changed. The big difference was with adults, whose time online zoomed from 10 to 19 hours a week (mainly because of increased online time at work). Maybe what keeps teens in place is the curfews; most parents put limits on their kids' computer time.

If stuck on a deserted island with one piece of functioning technology (not counting a fuelled airplane or a speedboat), most teens say the best thing to have would be a computer with Internet access (the local service provider on the island is offering reasonable bandwidth rates, we suppose), but many would prefer a television with cable service or a music player filled with their favourite tunes. Adults, who tend to be practical and therefore probably focus on how they would get off the island, overwhelmingly choose the Internet-enabled computer.

Seventy-five percent of Canadians who use the Internet reported receiving at least one unsolicited e-mail per week. The average weekly intake is about 130 unsolicited messages.

Spending Money

Teenagers each spend about $100 a year online, using their parent's credit card or, in a few cases, a parent's online purchasing account. They buy an average of three-and-a-half items, which usually include a video game, an electronic gadget, or clothing. One out of ten teens bought a book. If you take all teenagers into account, including those who spend a ton and those who don't buy a single thing, the average amount is more like $238. That's because about 10% of teens are charging more than $500 worth of online purchases. Only 6% of teens tell us they spent nothing online last year. The most common reasons for this are that parents won't allow it or that teens don't have a credit card.

Imagine That

Ten random but fortunately representative teenagers, five boys and five girls, are sitting on a bench. (It's a long bench. Okay, it's two benches.) We ask them what they get up to online.

- One never chats, plays online games, or visits a social network.
- Five play games with others.
- Three of the boys and four of the girls chat online.

- Nine of them use instant messaging when they're at home and want to communicate with friends. Only seven regularly use their home telephone line.
- Four of them have encountered someone online who wanted to meet them in person. Three of these four would be girls. These invitations aren't necessarily romantic, though; the online stranger could be another teenage girl.

The nice thing about the Internet, from the point of view of a teenager who doesn't have a credit card, is that you can get free stuff, particularly music and movies. Two-thirds of teenagers download music, and most of them use a peer-to-peer service that gives them songs free of charge. Paying for music has been getting more popular, though—between 2004 and 2007, the number of teens who paid for their downloads tripled. Most teens still buy CDs sometimes, too. The most common reason teenagers give for not pilfering music for free off the Internet is that their parents won't allow it. The other explanations we hear are that teens worry about downloading a virus, or they think getting free copies of commercial songs is immoral.

WHERE ARE THE GEEKS?

It's normal that part of your social life exists on the computer. It's normal for an adult to play video games. More than a third of Canadians share digital photos online instead of bothering to print them out. These activities no longer count as geeky.

But this doesn't mean the geeks have disappeared—they're still out there on the front lines of digital technology while the rest of us struggle to catch up. Stop a Canadian at random on the street and (after you've introduced yourself and explained why you stopped them) they'll probably tell you that they're no expert on high-tech. Only one in five Canadians claims to be very skilled with technology, and even though online activities are part of almost everyone's life now, the number of Canadians who view themselves as very skilled with the Internet increased by only 5% during the first decade of this century. The standard for what is considered very skilled has leaped up, along with the requirements for true geek status. More than a third of Canadians complain they can barely keep up with the speed of technological advance, and a further 20% see themselves falling way behind. Even those who have stayed ahead of the game admit it's a constant battle to stay on top. Half of Canadian adults rely on family members, friends, and printed newspapers to keep them abreast of changes in technology rather than on online reports, blogs, and so on.

In dealing with technological change,
are you ahead of the curve or dropping behind?

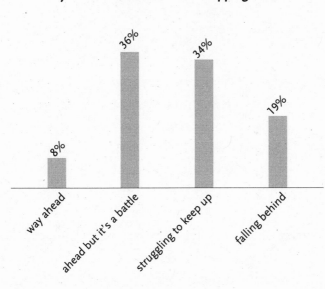

Forty percent of Canadian adults played a video game last month (that's twice as many as those who still use a camera that contains a roll of film). Among these game players, one-third play every day. Women seem to outplay men very slightly; women head to their gaming consoles an average of 16.3 times per month, compared to

15.3 times for men. In the overall population, though, men are still more likely to own a video game, and 45% have their own console, as compared to 31% of women. But it's certainly not the case that Canada's gaming population is overwhelmingly male—women make up a big portion of the pie.

Adults who played video games this month

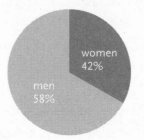

AGED ADDICTS

Among those who regularly play video games, it's actually the older gamers who are the most hardcore. Half of the gamers over the age of 55 play every single day, compared to just a quarter of the adult gamers under 55. Overall, older players head to the console an average of 20 times a month compared to just 15 times for younger players.

Gamers with less money spend more time on their consoles, playing roughly 17 times a month, compared to rich gamers, who play 13 times a month. Unlike rich gamers, lower-income gamers are usually recent converts who started playing in the last year or two or stopped playing for a long time and then took up the hobby again. Fifty percent of the rich players enjoyed their first video game between the ages of two and 10, compared to 35% of the lower-income players.

An even starker difference exists between the ages at which men and women started gaming. Most adult males were less than 10 years old when they started playing video games. Most women gamers were at least 20 when they took up this hobby.

OLD BUT WIRED

It's no surprise that the oldest Canadians spend less time online and are the least inclined to go beyond e-mails into the more advanced online activities.

Most older people don't consider the Internet an important part of their daily lives, and even those who use their computers regularly spend about a third less time on them than younger adults.

Older people aren't interested in watching live television from around the world on their computer. Younger people are. One in five younger Canadians, one in ten middle-aged, and one in twenty older Canadians might want to start their own video blog. But the fact that people of all ages respond enthusiastically to "making and sharing videos with friends and family online" raises the suspicion that most don't really understand what video blogging is—since the two phrases could describe the same activity! Older people are seven times more likely to say they'd like to make videos and share them online with friends and family than they are to express any interest in video blogging.

MYTH-BUSTER

Older adults are no less likely than young ones to use e-mail. In fact, 87% of over-55s say they communicate online regularly, compared to 90% of 18 to 34-year-olds. (In the language of opinion polls, that counts as a tie.)

"I download or listen to music online."

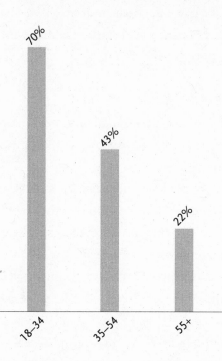

70%

43%

22%

18–34   35–54   55+

THE FUTURE IS NOW

We don't use people's tech-savvy credentials to divide up their answers on broader questions about how they see the country, what values seem important to them, and so on. We haven't yet looked into whether people with an e-mail addiction are especially likely to skip breakfast, sleep naked, or support gun control. This kind of thing might not be so far off, though. Marketers on radio and TV stations already pay very close attention to the people who like to be constantly online, as do politicians and media pundits. The thoughts and characteristics that mark a typical wired Canadian may soon be the subject of as much investigation as those of the average parent, wealthy person, or Saskatchewaner.

16 / THE WORKER

There may be days for each of us when we'd rather bang on a drum all day than go to work, days when the last person we want to see is our boss, and weeks or even years when it seems like far too long since our last holiday. Thousands of Canadian workers with little money to spare after paying the bills regularly drop handfuls of dollars into corner-store lottery games, despite the extreme odds against winning much money this way, in the hopes of a win that would allow them to take a trip or enjoy a luxury item that their regular paycheques would never allow. And yet, when we ask people to tell us about their work life and their employers, the most common stories are remarkably positive. We hear about workers who say they wouldn't quit even if they won a huge fortune in the lottery. We hear about bosses who are a pleasure to report to. The Canadian worker, by and large, is a happy beast, and the Canadian boss more often than not enjoys the love and respect of employees.

But we knew this rosy picture could not be the whole story. After listening to and duly noting the contentment professed by most people, we probed with more penetrating questions. Sure enough, people soon admitted to the stresses, the complaints, the hurt feelings, and the dashed hopes. It turns out we all harbour mixed emotions about the way we make our livings. So if you don't fit the picture-perfect image of the satisfied worker or the beloved boss, don't be alarmed.

WHAT ELSE IS THERE?

Loyalty is easy to profess. Workers immediately express loyalty to their workplace, with most declaring this loyalty to be strong. Unfortunately for bosses, it's not the sort of strong loyalty that stands up to, say, a better job offer from a rival. As soon as we dangled the prospect of a better-paying, similar job with a competitor, most people's loyalty crumbled. Seven out of ten claimed they'd reject the offer and stay with their current employer.

Even without the pay increase, workers don't seem to be as loyal as they pronounce themselves to be. Most people express an interest in changing jobs, and only half of these employees would prefer to remain with the same company—the other half would rather change employers as well. So what's an employer to do when faced with this instantly vanishing staff loyalty?

One idea some HR managers might want to ponder is offering extended health benefits so that employees can receive free massages or perhaps a hot-stone, deep-tissue treatment to ease their shoulder tension during the workday or whenever they want. That ought to buy a bit of solid loyalty, right? Or, how about a nice long vacation? That seems like a great idea to get workers onside. Or maybe workers really want to feel that they hold a stake in a company, rather than just being hired hands, so a good boss might curry their favour by offering profit-sharing incentives. And it's probably important for workers to know that a better paycheque could be just around the corner, along with a cushier job, so a system of promotions and rewards for reliable workers would be a real carrot, right? Wrong—apparently the main incentive for workers nowadays is money.

Percentage of Canadian workers who estimate it costs less than $20,000 per year to pay for an employee's health plan: 95%. Percentage who would swap their benefits for $20,000 per year: 38%.

Sure, we'd expect to see income brought up as a desirable feature of any new contract, but what stands out is how much this factor leaves all the others in the dust. By the way, another quirk of Canadian workers is that if you offer them $20,000 per year in exchange for their employee health benefits plan, they say no (even though these same people estimate the cost of a health plan is between $5,000 and $10,000 per worker).

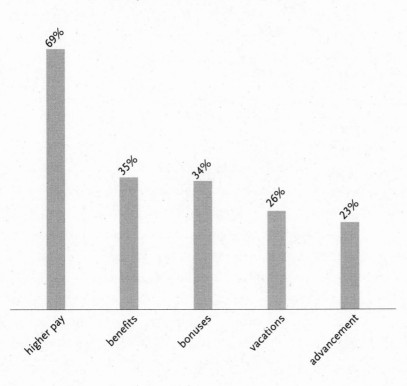

The top five incentives for employees

THE NORMAL WORKER

Ever feel like a drudge, a cog in a machine, just one more brick in the wall? We hope not. It's probably better for your self-esteem and sense of individuality not to resemble the average Canadian worker too closely. In order to avoid this, of course, we need to know what the typical worker is like, so that we can all figure out how to be at least a bit different!

THE AVERAGE CANADIAN WORKING MAN

He's worked for 5.8 employers (that job for four-fifths of an employer was probably the toughest). He joined his current company 9 years ago, and expects to stay for another 12 years, 1 month, and 5 days. If he could change careers completely, he might pick something in construction or IT. His resumé is out of date because he doesn't keep it ready and armed for new job opportunities. He did not apply for a new job last year. He's about 70% convinced that he has what it takes to succeed in the workplace for the next decade. He works full-time and earns $23 an hour. He wants more money.

THE AVERAGE CANADIAN WORKING WOMAN

She's had 4.8 employers, and she's worked for her current one for 7 years, 8 months, and 12 days. (If this statistic makes you feel shockingly average, perhaps it would be better to put this book down for now and read it tomorrow instead.) She plans to stay with her current employer for another 10 years and 6 months. A new job in a hotel or a hospital might well appeal to her. Her resumé is also not quite up to date. She claims to be more loyal to her employer than the average male worker does, but she's just as likely to take another job if someone offers her more money. She's about 65% sure that she can succeed in the workplace and, unlike her male counterpart, is more interested in health and benefits coverage than the prospect of cash bonuses for hard work. She works full-time and earns $19 an hour.

OUT OF FIVE TYPICAL CANADIAN WORKERS . . .

- two struggle to balance work and family time, complaining that one of these suffers because of the other.
- two admit to being burned out.
- three wish they could work less.

- one and a half say they've got their dream job.
- one and a half are on the lookout for another job.
- four like their boss.

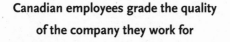

Canadian employees grade the quality of the company they work for

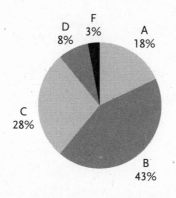

D
8%

F
3%

A
18%

C
28%

B
43%

WHAT'S THE MONEY FOR?

If money is time, and free money is free time, then it's an odd quirk of these otherwise average workers that they wouldn't quit their jobs if someone handed them enough money to retire immediately. Instead, they'd take the money and spend only part of it on free time—meaning that they'd cut their work hours down—but continue to toil part-time. The exception is the average workers who are older than 70 and have not yet retired. As you might guess, these elderly employees are more likely to say they'd quit.

Many people want to switch to government, entertainment, or consultancy. Fewer people want to switch to banking, accounting, or financial services.

"If I could, I'd quit completely."

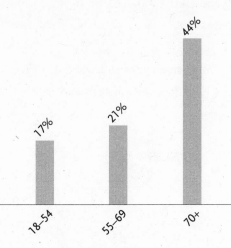

But, as you might not guess (unless you're extremely good at guessing), the over-70s are also much more likely to say they'd continue to work just as hard as before, even with all the money they need to retire.

"I'd keep working without even reducing my hours."

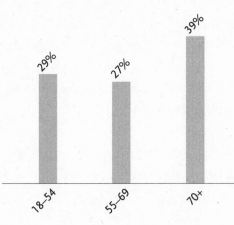

Big Prize Win for YOU!
Maybe the idea of enough money to retire isn't exciting enough for some of us. When we ask people to imagine having this kind of wealth, less than one in five say it would make them quit their jobs completely.

If we raise the excitement factor and ask someone to imagine they've just won $5 million, then they're much more likely to want to quit work. More than one in three of the people we talked to said they'd never work another day if they won such a prize.

WHY I CAN'T RETIRE

We asked workers over 55 why they hadn't retired yet. They told us they needed more money and also wanted to stay active. It was less common to say they were in it for the social life, and less common still to say it was all for the love of the job (only one-fifth of them said this).

Older workers, on average, want six and a half weeks of vacation every year. More than half plan to keep working past the age of 65, with a quarter expecting to work full-time for as long as possible.

> **Two out of five working men regularly
> put in more than 40 hours per week.
> Only one in five working women do this.**

DOES ANYONE ACTUALLY USE RED TAPE?

Whoever first decided to use red ribbon to tie up important documents in 16th-century England must have thought it a simple, attractive, and practical method for keeping papers together. Little did he or she know that it would remain a reviled symbol long after the invention of paper clips and three-ring binders.

Canadian workers say that red tape is the biggest barrier keeping them from getting their jobs done. (We assume very few of these workers are talking about tape literally, although it's true that it can be tricky to work with, especially when static electricity causes it to stick to your fingers.) Almost half of those employed full-time complain that red tape represents a significant burden for them. Men complain about this more commonly than women. Public-sector workers whine slightly more than private-sector ones, but not by much.

After all that tape, the biggest hassles to workers' ability to get the job done include unclear expectations (four in ten suffer from this), office politics (a problem for one-third of us), and gossip. Whether it's time given to gossiping about others, or time spent wondering if others are gossiping about us, this impedes the ability of three out of every ten employees to do their best work.

**Out of every twenty Canadian employees,
one hates his or her job.**

It's More Than a Mood

Depression, of the clinical sort that won't go away and prevents people from feeling content on a sunny day, affects 14% of Canadians to the extent that they've gone to a doctor, described their state of mind, and been diagnosed with the mental illness. This translates into 11% of workers, 20% of non-workers, 11% of men, and 18% of women. If you add to that group the much larger gang (22% of Canadians and 19% of workers) who think they're depressed but haven't got a medical diagnosis, then almost 33% of the entire workforce feels locked in a wrestling match with their own dark moods. Almost everyone has heard that depression, left untreated, can be life threatening. Only 33% of respondents had a hard time distinguishing between the illness and simply being in a sad mood.

If it seems odd that 20% of Canadian workers carry out their jobs every day in the belief that they suffer from a potentially dangerous mental illness without ever seeking medical help, bear in mind people's attitudes towards depression. Even though it has become rare to scoff that the condition is something people ought to snap out of and most people recognize that depression should be treated seriously, this growing attitude of respect for its seriousness certainly doesn't mean an improvement in attitude towards depression sufferers. If anything, the label "mental illness" stigmatizes depressives even further, so that getting a medical diagnosis can be a scary thing in itself. Half the employees we spoke to agreed that if someone in their workplace suffered from depression to the point of needing to miss work days, they'd probably get in trouble and maybe lose their job. The vast majority—80%—believe that co-workers who are diagnosed with depression will probably keep it to themselves out of fear of hurting their future opportunities at work.

As a reminder of how tricky public opinion can be, however, when we conducted another survey asking employees to rate their companies' general supportiveness when it came to health issues, four out of five described their employers as accommodating.

SICK WITH STRESS
Two out of five workers blame stress in the workplace for making them physically ill. More women than men reported this. Incidentally, women are also more likely to say stress in the home and in personal life makes them sick—three in ten experience this, compared to fewer than one in four men.

Only one in five people say that their workplace has guidelines on how to deal with employees who are suffering from stress, depression, or some form of mental illness. Even for the most conscientious worker there really is no one person or place to turn to (and it's clear that the majority of workers don't want to have anything to do with the HR department when a stress illness arises). This is a really serious issue in the workplace, and if it weren't for people like Bill Wilkerson, who started the non-profit Roundtable on Mental Health and Addiction, or former senator Michael Kirby, now chair of the Mental Health Commission of Canada, or a few other enlightened beings, many more managers and workers alike would be pretending that these illnesses are isolated to a handful of people in every workplace. As it is, support levels are extremely high for programs in the workplace to help employees with mental health issues, the understanding and empathy is great, the desire for CEO leadership is palpable, and mental illness is the worst-kept workplace secret going. If only these factors led to more action, it would be an incredible achievement.

WELL WORKERS

Employees with health plans think more highly of the companies they work for. Almost all workers say that if they really believed their employer cared about their health, they'd be less likely to seek work elsewhere. They also feel an obligation to keep to a minimum the costs of health benefit plans by staying healthy so as not to require treatment. People who work for bigger companies say their employers offer health education, and most employees approve of employers taking an interest in a worker's health as long as this doesn't involve nosing into the worker's health information. It's one thing to have the company hand out anti-stress balls and give tips on the top ten ways to keep your brain young, but quite another to take notice of an employee's high blood pressure and advise this individual not to eat donuts on morning break. Still, roughly one-third of Canadians do not have a problem with employers actively helping them to manage their health, even if this gives the boss access to personal health information.

> **Most workers worry that they may be at risk of getting cancer, heart disease, or diabetes. Not many are concerned about the prospect of obesity or mental illness.**

Two-thirds of employees who receive benefits give top marks to their company's health plan. This is more than double the high-approval rating for Canada's health care system overall. The best thing about these plans, say workers, is that they pay for drugs and dental work.

PRINTING CRIMES

Okay, time for the really serious problem in today's workplace. Two-thirds of office workers print personal material on the office printer or copy personal documents on the company photocopier. The most common personal materials sent to the office printers are:

- driving directions
- resumés
- photos

While waiting for their personal documents to print, half of the workers will either stare off into space and do nothing, or stand next to the printer snooping into other documents that are waiting to be collected.

VACATION TIME

Even though the idea of more vacation days appeals to many workers, the fact is that a large proportion of employees don't even take the vacation days they're already entitled to. One in four employed women and three in ten men spend some of their allotted vacation days at work. A common reason given by these people is that they leave it until too late to schedule vacation time, and then it becomes impossible to leave work at short notice, so the vacation days just stack up and in the end get converted into extra money. (In fact, one in ten employed people say they deliberately don't take vacation days in order to receive the extra income.) It's very rare—though certainly not unheard of in our surveys—for employees to admit they're scared to use their vacation days because doing so would annoy their boss and so jeopardize their job.

HOLIDAY GUILT

Young employees take, on average, two weeks of vacation per year. Middle-aged employees take two and a half weeks. Older employees take three. Employees between the ages of 35 and 54 are the most likely to work more than 40 hours per week and to have cancelled or postponed vacations because of work. Young employees are the most likely to feel guilty when they take time (even legitimate vacation time) off work.

Twenty-five percent of employed men have cancelled or postponed vacations because of work. Twenty percent of them check their work e-mail and voicemail while on vacation. Employed women are half as likely to do either of these things.

Thirty percent of women say they feel guilty when they take vacations from work. This might wear off with increasing age, though— older workers are much less likely than young adults to express feelings of guilt about taking time off. Twenty percent of working women complain that their employer's vacation policy is unfair, and even more say that their boss doesn't encourage them to use all the vacation days allotted. Fifty percent of the workers we spoke to agreed that technology has made it harder to get away from work, although there is a flip side for some; roughly 20% of men say that having a cellphone or other communications gizmo allows them to take vacations more easily. In any case, most workers ignore their gadgets and cellphones completely when they go on vacation.

When asked whether they experience envy when a co-worker returns from vacation, most young people say yes. Most older workers don't understand this question at all. (Of course, one might think the time to experience envy is when a co-worker is leaving on vacation, not afterwards when they're stuck at work again!)

People use their vacation days to attend a wedding, a family reunion, and so on. Most employees also point out that more important than the occasion for a vacation is the ability to afford a vacation. It's less common to say that thoughts of an amazing destination or convenient travel options would prompt a vacation.

What would encourage employees to take a holiday? Between 20 and 25% of workers agree that they might go on more vacations if company policy required at least a minimum vacation time. A similar proportion of employees say they would get away more often if they had a lighter workload, a more encouraging boss, a fair vacation policy, and greater confidence that management approved of vacations. But the most popular answer we got was that none of these factors would encourage people to leave work. For most employees, holidays are all about seeing family and scraping together the money to do so. What the company's vacation policy dictates is not as important.

Ottawans are much more likely than Victorians or Haligonians to say they work primarily because they enjoy it, rather than because work pays for the rest of their life. People in those coastal cities usually see work as a means to an end.

Most Canadian workers manage to achieve that great state of equilibrium known as the work/life balance. Older workers do this with greater aplomb and success than younger adults, who are more likely to struggle. A quarter of young workers feel their careers suffer from their inability to balance work and life properly. Older people—that is, older than 55—enjoy their work; younger people don't, or at least, not enough to lift their work life beyond the status of a means to pay the bills.

TRUSTED PROFESSIONALS

A firefighter could walk into a random gathering of one hundred Canadians, who, like many of the random groups mentioned in this book, happen to perfectly represent the whole population of this country, and introduce himself to almost anyone. That person would immediately trust him. Eighty-one people at the party would likely give the firefighter their highest level of trust, the sort usually reserved for (reliable) family members. A judge also attending the gathering might meet two people who view her job with suspicion before she encounters two more who genuinely respect the work she does. That's because this party would be split fifty-fifty, with half the guests trusting Canada's judiciary.

If a car salesman showed up at this party, he might wander around, drink in hand, constantly introducing himself to people, only to be met with narrowed eyes and dubious expressions. In fact, he'd be best advised to lie and say he was a firefighter. Only one person at the party completely trusts car salespeople—perhaps it's the salesman himself.

On the other hand, since this particular salesman has pragmatically decided to call himself a firefighter, he's apparently wise enough not to trust himself, meaning that someone else at the party is the one who most respects his integrity. This presents the sad prospect that, at some point during this party, the poor car salesman will introduce himself to that rare salesperson-trusting character, start talking about his fictional life as a firefighter, and receive the cold shoulder unjustly from the one person in the room who doesn't believe a word that firefighters say but would bet his house on the advice of anyone who sells cars for a living.

Also wandering around the room in a struggle to find a few people to respect her might be a national politician (who would need to meet a lot of people before encountering the two individuals who consider her extremely trustworthy), a local politician (looking for the four people who really trust him), a chief executive officer (who might meet four people who trust her completely and another seventeen who'd usually give her the benefit of the doubt), and a home builder. If your job involves building new homes, you might be alarmed to know that most Canadians doubt your word. Six people at this party would consider you entirely reliable, while a further seventeen would think you tell the truth most of the time.

> **Canadians intuitively trust soldiers but not priests, nurses but not plumbers, accountants but not mechanics, daycare workers but not real estate agents. Most people express suspicion towards the environmental movement; only 40% consider it trustworthy.**

LEAGUE OF TRUSTWORTHINESS: INDUSTRIES

When a company issues a statement, we're inclined to judge it according to how trustworthy the entire industry seems. Here's a list of industries—the most trusted are at the top, the least trusted at the bottom.

- medical research
- airlines
- tech companies
- tourism

- food
- drugs and pharmaceuticals
- banks
- restaurants
- financial planning
- retail stores
- radio stations/shows
- investment advisors
- cable TV stations/shows
- brewers
- hydroelectric power
- household product makers
- liquor sellers
- newspapers
- television
- automobile manufacturers
- long-distance telephone service providers
- advertising
- oil
- tobacco

THE LIFE PLAN

We suggested to a group of 1,000 Canadians that certain people or things had had an impact on their choice of career or their decision to change jobs. We then gave them a list of possible sources of such impacts:

- a parent
- a relative/friend/neighbour
- a newspaper
- a co-worker/associate
- a government employment centre

- a high school teacher
- a particular mentor
- a guidance counsellor
- an Internet-based career site

And it went on, and on . . . the long list probably tried the patience of many of the people surveyed!

"Yes, an Internet job site was helpful."

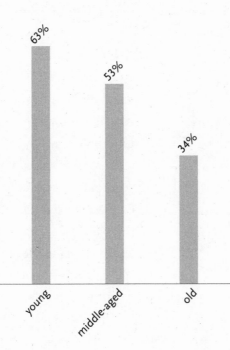

Most young people credited Internet sites and guidance counsellors with affecting their careers. Most people over 55 did not mention these resources, presumably because they weren't available earlier. Another interesting difference is that almost all young adults mentioned their parents as influential to their career, while only three-quarters of older people said the same.

Among those who did experience some sort of career influence from a parent, 32% of young adults described the influence as very helpful, compared to 19% of middle-aged people and 23% of older respondents. Of older Canadians overall, 60% say their parents didn't get involved in their choice of job or career path. These older respondents are also much more likely to regret not getting professional career planning or more job-related information earlier in life. The people over 55 who tried using an Internet job site at some point to help their career path generally did not find it helpful. Younger people did.

"I've experienced a moment when a parent influenced my career choices."

95%

75%

18-34   55+

ANOTHER BRICK IN THE WALL?

We heard all that stuff from people who grind out their work every day to get a paycheque. But we figured it must feel different to get that paycheque when you own the company, or at least when you get to boss everybody else around. One way to stop feeling like a brick in the wall is . . . to stop being a brick and start being the bricklayer! At least, that's what a motivational speaker might tell you. But how different are the lives of people at the top of the workplace pile? To find out, we went and talked to the boss.

THE BOSS

The boss works longer hours. People who work as managers put in an average of 44 hours per week, compared to the 37 hours put in by their underlings. Managers also take fewer sick days—just two and a half per year, compared to the three days and three hours taken by non-managers.

Compensating for the extra workload is the feeling of power and independence that comes with giving orders rather than taking them, and that drive for freedom lures many from the corporate world into the havens of small business operation. The small-business owners we talked to speak warmly of leaping off the corporate ladder. They commonly say the appeal is twofold—losing one's boss and gaining a better work/life balance. Slightly less than half of small-business owners ticked the boxes for "following my passion" or "working on a new idea" when asked to pick the best reasons to start their own business. Only about a quarter of these entrepreneurs thought the promise of more money lured people away from a safer career path. Women are less likely than men to say that income was a major factor in wanting to start their own business. More often, women say they wanted flexible work hours so as to manage family commitments.

This picture changes somewhat when we ask these business owners what they hope for the future. The "be my own boss" answer is still extremely popular, but the prospect of working fewer hours or spending more time on vacation drops off. Most of all, people focus on the goal of making more money and liking the work they do.

According to Statistics Canada, roughly one in seven Canadian workers are self-employed.

Self-bossing bosses report that mastering technology is among the most important skills for running your business, particularly those technologies that keep a person up to date with timely information, promote the business, and help reach new customers. Almost everyone uses computers, word processors, spreadsheets, and basic

Internet software, and roughly half of business owners have set up a network of laptops and desktops on a shared server. A quarter of business owners proudly claim to be at the sophisticated tech level, with complicated networks that mix their mobile gadgets into the same system as their computers, working with high-end specialized software.

Most business owners feel that they're saving about half an hour a day by using mobile technology to get work done while on the road. A tiny fraction think their mobile devices save them at least three hours a day. When we asked business owners what they'd like technology to do for them, the most common answer was to allow them to be better organized. This desire outstripped the need to make documents look more professional, to speed up work times, to improve communication, or to make financial management easier.

PLACES WHERE BUSINESS OWNERS HAVE TAKEN A PHONE CALL

- sitting in traffic—three in five
- taking care of a child—one in four
- in a grocery store—two in five
- on a family excursion—three in ten
- at the cottage—three in ten
- on the golf course—one in ten
- in the washroom—one in four
- in bed—one in three
- at dinner with significant other—one in two

WHO MAKES THE LEAP?

Those who start their own businesses often worked as corporate bosses or managers beforehand. Out of every ten small-business owners, two used to be executives, two were some other kind of professional, one was a secretary or clerk, one worked in sales, another did technical work, and another was a self-described "blue collar" worker. That leaves two others. One might have been a farmer, a fisher, or a student, but chances are they both listed their background as "Other."

WHO'S THE BOSS?
Among those small-business operators who hire employees, two out of five employ their spouse. It's also common to give a job to your children; one in ten men and one in seven women do this. Women are twice as likely to hire a sibling. In fact, if you're a woman who owns her own business, chances are you've hired your husband, a child, a parent, another family member, an in-law, a friend, or a roommate. If you're a man, you probably haven't done this.

WORDS OF WISDOM
We asked Canadian business owners to tell us about the difficulties they faced after they decided to become their own boss. Here are the top five challenges they faced in the early days of their projects:

1. finding clients
2. keeping a steady workload
3. working too many hours
4. dealing with bureaucracy and regulations
5. scraping together enough money

We spoke with 2,253 small-business operators to find out what they thought were the biggest challenges in working for themselves. Only one individual replied that the hardest thing to overcome was procrastination. (You know who you are.)

And here are the top ten suggestions for aspiring business owners:

1. Know your competition.
2. Develop a good business plan.
3. Research the market.
4. Network and develop alliances (but be careful of the free booze at business networking events).*
5. Take time for marketing.
6. Seek mentors.
7. Spend less time worrying about the "look" of business cards, etc., and more time on defining the needs you meet.
8. Survey potential customers.**
9. Do your homework when considering where to locate your business.
10. Join clubs and associations.

EXPERIENCE HURTS

One jarring statistic we found when talking to business owners is that the older ones who'd been at it for longer were much more likely to say they used a backup tool to ensure their business records were safely stored. The majority of business owners under the age of 35 do not do this. (Perhaps they're still waiting to experience that first awful moment of a damaging system crash and data loss?)

The younger owners lead the older ones, however, in appreciating the usefulness of what's called collaborative technology—70% express enthusiasm about how this helps employees work together and contribute to each other's achievements. The younger owners agree that

---

*Our editor insisted on adding the last part of this tip. We understand it to be based on personal experience.

**Perhaps this would be a good moment to point out that here at Ipsos we do some really excellent market-research work.

young employees generally seem more keyed up about the new technologies, whereas older workers don't tackle it with such gusto. Older business owners aren't so sure about this perception—only half agree with it. Older business owners agree that more experienced employees have greater business savvy while younger ones are more tech-savvy. Younger bosses don't like this statement.

Mistakes Were Not Made

Remarkably, when we ask experienced small-business owners whether they'd do anything differently if they were to start a business all over again, most say no.

Of course, this group is by definition fairly successful because they're still in business. Presumably we'd get a different answer from people whose businesses had not survived the early stages.

Among those who admitted they'd do some things differently, the most common complaint was that they wish they'd started younger. The next most common complaint was that they wish they'd sought more financial advice.

Clocking Out

Phew! That was hard work. Time for a reward! After a hard day at the office, on the worksite, or even at home in front of the computer, it's time for some pleasure. The next chapter is about the bedroom. Turn the page to find out who's waiting there.

17 / The Sexual Canadian

Single people in their twenties are not really single. Yes, they might feel single, especially after a painful breakup, or while still awaiting that first full-on adult romance that brings with it promises of marriage and lifelong happiness. They may, of course, experience emotions of loneliness, excitement, frustration, and elation; it's even possible for twenty-somethings to swear off love forever, as though romance has, for them, been a long, arduous, and ultimately doomed saga finally arriving at its sombre conclusion.

But that's just a superficial state of affairs. To be truly, profoundly single, people must at least have passed their thirtieth birthday, and really ought to be closer to 45. That's why, in our survey of the romantic and sexual practices of singles, we focused on Canadians aged 30 and older who were either widowed, divorced, separated, or otherwise unattached. Here's what we found out . . .

Single People Go on Dates

All right, this one is no shocker. What's very clear, though, is that the image of the dating single person best describes that younger group— the ones who haven't yet hit 45. The proportion of single people who date falls steeply as the years go by.

More men go on dates than women (bear in mind, though, that the people least likely to date are elderly widowed Canadians, who are mostly women), and single university graduates are more likely to date than less-educated single people. And if your last major breakup was more than four years ago, you may well have stopped dating, or at least be taking a long break—half of those who did not break up with somebody in the last four years did not go on any dates either.

"I'm single, and I've been on a date in the last four years."

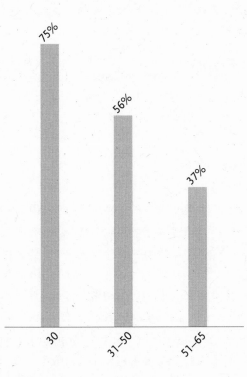

DIVORCED PEOPLE USE THE INTERNET

We hear about Internet dating mostly from divorced people, or those who describe themselves as separated rather than single. And many of the widowed Canadians we spoke with told us they've used online dating websites. For this survey, only 60 of the widowed people we spoke with were actively dating, so we can't really be sure they speak for widowed Canadians everywhere. Still, it caught our eye that 20 of these people—one out of every three—were using Internet dating sites. The people who see themselves as single rather than being half of a former relationship are the least likely to use Internet dating; only a quarter of them do, roughly the same number as those who have found dates at bars or clubs or through their work. The most popular way to find love is to go on a date with a friend of a friend. The least popular paths that were mentioned were through church, religious outings, and neighbours.

One-quarter of Canadians have never celebrated Valentine's Day.

THE DEAL-BREAKER

Given the choice between sleeping with an unpleasant person who is disease-free and sleeping with a lovely person who suffers from herpes, it seems that most single people would choose the one they don't like very much. Women, especially, are more likely to say that their primary concern with a new sexual partner is the possibility of contracting a disease. Issues like compatibility, character traits, honesty, and physical attraction are way down the list. As for worries about whether this new sexual partner wants a long-term relationship, well, forget it. First, the STD issue needs to be settled.

It doesn't matter which STD we're talking about (well, on some level, of course, it does, because people inevitably consider the deadly or disfiguring illnesses worse than the unnoticeable ones) because by far the strongest reaction to the topic of STDs is that single people want none of them and won't have sex with an infected person regardless of which infection it is. The term STD is the biggest turnoff in the dating scene.

That's why, before having sex with a new person, most women ask their soon-to-be lover for reassurance, saying something along the lines of, "You don't have any STDs, do you?" It's also why almost nobody asks about specific diseases. Less than one in ten single people say they asked their last sexual partner about genital herpes, for instance. Even fewer asked about syphilis, chlamydia, gonorrhea, or something less common. Some people do ask about HIV, but even this famous illness comes up in only about one out of every six or seven of these awkward conversations.

Women are more afraid of herpes than men, possibly because they know the disease in women can cause pregnancy problems and birth defects (although this is rare). Four out of ten women even say they're generally afraid of getting involved with someone new because they could pick up this disease. Three out of four men say they're not afraid. Interestingly, these general fears run stronger among less-educated people—only a quarter of university graduates think herpes is a major danger of starting a new relationship.

In heterosexual couples, it's usually the woman who broaches the topic of sexual diseases— men are extremely likely not to ask.

Given that most doctors don't test for herpes, and herpes "sufferers" usually don't experience any symptoms, there's a great big hole in the logic here for most single people: they claim they won't have sex with a herpes sufferer, but they will accept the vague phrase "I was tested for STDs and didn't have any of them" as a good enough assurance to green-light the rest of a steamy night! Most of the time, when single people start having sex, they haven't acquired any information about their new partner's possible relationship with the herpes virus.

Most sexually active Canadians do not always use condoms. One-quarter use them most of the time, one-sixth say it's just some of the time, and another quarter never use them.

Men and women, old and young—everyone agrees that genital herpes is a fact of life and that sufferers should be honest with their prospective partners (most of whom will promptly dump them, according to our polls). The vast majority also agree that other people cannot be trusted to admit that they've been infected,* and that asking them specifically is an extremely uncomfortable experience. The majority of women (and half the men) regretfully agree that if they were on the brink of having a relationship with someone they really liked and then found out that the person was infected with herpes, this knowledge would completely scupper the relationship.

Of course, since this survey was done in North America, most people we asked already carry herpes in one form or another (such as cold sores) and have no idea that this is the case. By the time North Americans reach the age of 50 years, almost 90% have developed antibodies to herpes, meaning they have been exposed to it one way or another.

WHAT THEY DIDN'T TEACH US IN SCHOOL
Whereas people with no post-secondary education can accurately guess that the proportion of Canadians who carry genital herpes is between one-fifth and one-quarter of the population, those with post-secondary schooling tend to underestimate how common the disease is—on average, these people think that one-sixth of Canadians carry it.

TEENS
People between the ages of 14 and 17 know a bit about sex. Half a million of them say they've had it, roughly one out of three. One out of four of those teens didn't use a condom last time. Seven out of ten

---

*And they're correct not to trust people—not so much because of dishonesty but because most folks don't know.

of them engaged in unprotected oral sex, often unaware that diseases get transmitted this way. One out of five teens overall think mutual masturbation counts as sexual intercourse. (Nearly one out of three adult mothers agree.)

Among those sexually active half-million teens, the average number of partners is three. If you ask six of the teens to describe their current or most recent sexual relationship, only five of them will say their partner was monogamous. The other one knew their partner was having sex with someone else during the same period. Most don't know that chlamydia can cause infertility or that genital warts are related to cervical cancer. ·

Fewer than one out of four teens find their school's sex education classes useful. Most admit that their own feelings of awkwardness and embarrassment keep them from getting all the information they need.

Teenagers say their main role models for sexual relationships are their parents, not movie stars or musicians. Despite this, four out of ten teenagers aged 14 to 17 have not spoken with their mothers about sex and sexuality.

Boomers

People between the ages of 40 and 64 spend an average of 20 minutes a day having sex or being romantic (as if those amount to same thing). They consider themselves more sexually liberated than their parents, and they believe their generation started a sexual revolution. The experience of, you know, doing it, makes them feel loved and appreciated, although most report that it can be ruined by fatigue, by stress, or by the lack of time left after meeting work and family obligations.

One-quarter of people in this age group complain that their partner is not adventurous. The same proportion say that menopause is getting in the way right now (either their own or a partner's). One-fifth feel too unattractive to have great sex, the usual complaint being

obesity. Only one person in ten, however, blames their partner's unat-
tractiveness or weight for their lack of great sex. Erection and ejac-
ulation problems afflict between one-fifth and one-quarter of men.
One in twenty say they can't have great sex because of their partner's
hygiene (or lack thereof).

Asked when their sex lives peaked, the most popular answer from
Boomers is their thirties. Ten percent say they're still waiting for their
sex lives to peak. They describe sex these days as intimate and tender,
in contrast to how it used to be in their twenties. In those days, it
was fun, spontaneous, and exciting. Forty-nine percent of Boomers
say they had an adventurous sex life in their twenties. Only 15% of
Boomers describe their current sex life this way. Seventeen percent of
Boomers describe their current sex lives as lonely.

Now you'd think the phrase "sowing your wild oats" would most
likely apply to those who spend their youth in the grain-bountiful prairie provinces of Manitoba, Saskatchewan, and Alberta. Alas, another
stereotype bites the dust. The Boomers who are most likely to say they
had a "wild" sex life in their twenties are Atlantic Canadians, who rise
to the label at 37%, compared to 32% of the people in the prairies.
Hence the new replacement phrase, "sowing your wild codpiece."

Boomers who described their sex life in their twenties as "wild."

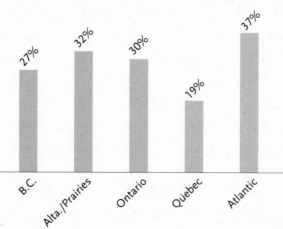

But then a pattern emerged when we looked at those Boomers who described their sex lives in their twenties as "reckless."

Boomers who described their sex lives in their twenties as "reckless."

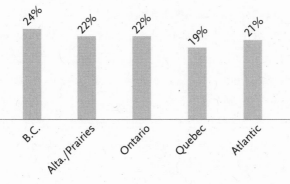

Generally, though, middle-aged lovers enjoy sex more than they used to, or say it's equally enjoyable. They say it's easier to please and satisfy their partner. While only half say their partner's ability to satisfy them has increased, another quarter say the satisfaction has stayed the same as the years have gone by. Only a quarter have noticed a drop in how sexy or satisfying their partner is today, compared to the partner(s) they knew during early adulthood.

If you're looking for some Boomer generation love, here's the breakdown of who's available and who's not:
- 62% of men and 54% of women are married.
- 13% of men and 14% of women are common-law.
- 5% of men and 7% of women are in a steady relationship.
- 6% of men and 11% of women are not looking for love.

So that leaves . . .
- 10% of men and 11% of women who are looking for love.

Plus, if you're the aggressive sort, you could try pursuing the 5% of men or the 4% of women who describe their dating relationship as casual.

STATE OF THE CANADIAN PENIS

Finally, since we're in the dirty part of this book, we may as well go all the way, so to speak, and report that middle-aged Canadian men are not entirely satisfied with their erections. Please be aware of this next time you speak to one.*

Only one-third of men between the ages of 40 and 65 announced to our hard-working pollsters that they are very satisfied with the overall quality of their you-know-what.

---

*That is, when you speak to a Canadian man. Not to an erection.

Governments probably seemed like a good idea at the time when nations were first invented. Back then, the effort required to gather public opinion on every issue would have bankrupted a country. Imagine holding elections—nationwide referenda—on every minute issue of policy when the fastest means of transport was a horse-drawn carriage! Morse code hadn't even been invented. So it's no wonder that, when early democrats demanded rule by the people, they kept their ambitions pretty modest. Nowadays, thanks mostly to hard-working opinion pollsters like us,* regular Canadians, average or otherwise, could easily run the country themselves using an online forum.

Of course, today's politicians aren't likely to push for such a sweeping change to our system of government. Even politicians who most often call for a referendum on any big issue would stop short of handing over power completely. What if Canada became the first country to really be ruled by its people? That is, if every opinion poll on a matter of policy actually determined the law, what kind of country would this become? Well, there's no need to imagine it, because this chapter tells you exactly what Canada, if it were a perfect democracy, would look like. (Hint: it would go broke pretty quickly.)

We, the People, Decree . . .

Protect our market.
Canadians want to increase domestic ownership of companies and

---

*This line became the subject of a bitter and irresolvable dispute with our editor.

property in this country. Most agree that foreign ownership is a problem. Not all of these people go as far as arguing that the current level of foreign control hurts our economy—just 37% sign their names to that accusation, while 18% say it has no impact one way or the other. It would be a tight vote, but among those willing to voice an opinion, the ones who think we need stricter rules outnumber those who think government is either too strict or about right in deciding what parts of our economy can be sold to foreigners.

Is the federal government too strict, not strict enough, or about right when it comes to regulating foreign investment and ownership?

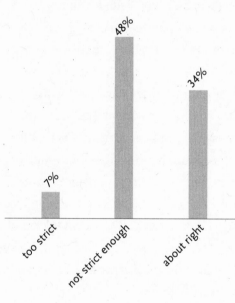

Elect the Senate.

The people would vote to change the Senate into an elected body. Of course, if the country were really being governed by opinion polls, the Houses of Parliament would lose their main reason for existing anyway.

Get a national energy policy.

Albertans beware! When the idea was suggested to voters everywhere, nine out of ten Canadians agreed that we should have a standard set of rules for how energy resources get harnessed across the country, how they are to be transported, and how they can be sold. A referendum on having a one-size-fits-all national energy policy would therefore have passed easily if Canada were governed by opinion poll.

Put photo radar everywhere.

We the people want cameras set up in school zones to take photographs of cars that break the speed limit. Every car's speed will be measured. Every offending driver will receive a fine in the mail. Eighty-four percent of us favour photo radar in these locations (60% strongly support it), so the minority opposition on this issue really doesn't stand a chance! We also want signs posted to warn drivers that they're being monitored and photographed (a two-thirds majority favours this).

We'll also install those cameras at intersections so that any vehicle travelling through a red light will get caught and the driver will receive a ticket. This vote would pass a national referendum with another solid majority—77%.

And don't think that, after quietly proceeding through the school zone and stopping at the red light, you'll be able to zoom away when you hit the highway. We want cameras there, too. There's 70% support for highway photo radar.

We won't dispatch more police to deal with traffic, however. With 50% of Canadians feeling that the level of police traffic enforcement is already about right (and 7% feeling it's too much), there's no majority for a "Yes" vote on increasing the number of cops out catching speeders.

Leave the seals alone.

The new Canadian government-by-poll would axe the seal hunt. No more clubbing baby seals. It's a divisive issue, for sure, with only a slim majority voting to end the practice on the Atlantic coast, and this law will appall the two-thirds of Atlantic Canadians who support the hunt. It might well lead to a referendum on sovereignty for the eastern provinces, although at the moment 85% of Atlantic Canadians want their region to stay part of Canada. Overall, 52% of Canadians would vote to ban the hunt, with 40% voting against such a bill, and the rest unsure.

Help people kill themselves, if they want.

Enough of forcing terminally ill people to stay with us to the bitter end! Seven in ten Canadians give their stamp of moral approval to doctor-assisted suicide in cases where a patient asks for help in ending their own life. In general terms, Canadians are even more emphatic: three-quarters of us recognize a right to die.

Hire more doctors and nurses.

Eighty percent of Canadians would feel more confident about the future of the health care system if the government hired more doctors and nurses (along with the other people who have jobs in hospitals, clinics, and so on). Ninety percent say it's important for political parties to address the doctor shortage.

We also want a webpage where we can see a list of standard wait times for operations and other procedures, as well as a guarantee that we'll get our treatment before that standard time is up. (This last policy would pass with a majority made up of two-thirds of the population, with just 16% opposed and the rest abstaining.)

Buy more buses.

Sixty percent of Canadians believe there is not enough funding from the various levels of government for public transit.

Support more schools.

Teachers in British Columbia would get a big boost from their pro-vincial opinion-poll government. An unbeatable majority of 87% in that province would vote for putting more money into public educa-tion, and not by selling or leasing out schools to private groups. The people dictate that school buildings must be well maintained, and school boards must offer stable and secure job opportunities to local people in need of work.

Endow more musicians.

Another bill to pass easily through the new nationwide parliament would be an increase to arts funding. Canadians agree in principle that cultural and arts events contribute to a local economy. In practice, a strong majority—60%—would vote for more cultural investments, to come out of local government budgets.

Fight AIDS overseas.

The generosity of the new government-by-poll would not stop at the Canadian border. We the people would also fight against HIV and AIDS worldwide. Ninety-one percent of Canadians feel it is impor-tant that we help people in developing countries get access to treat-ment. However, after all the money we spent on buses, musicians, and doctors, this international AIDS-fighting bill might not offer a generous new pile of cash for the charities working in Africa and elsewhere. Half of our population feels we already spend enough in this regard. (One in ten Canadians think we spend too much fighting AIDS already.) Sixty percent feel the disease has grown into a world-wide pandemic best described as an international emergency, which implies that plenty of voters must take the relaxed position that it's an emergency pandemic we're already spending enough to fix.

Keep private industry in its place.

We're happy to hire private companies to work at public recreation facilities, to complement public transit, and to develop roads and highways. However, in a national referendum, Canadians would vote against allowing the private sector a significant role in the operation of schools (68% say no), in hospitals (67% say no), or in providing water (62% say no), sewage treatment (57% say no), or electric power (58% say no).

Allow more facilities for drug addicts.

Fifty-five percent of Canadians believe safe injection sites are a good thing for the country, and half of us think they should expand to other cities beyond Vancouver. Only 40% oppose these facilities, where drug addicts can go to inject themselves with illegal narcotics in a controlled and monitored setting with clean needles supplied. Under such a policy, the injection sites would be specially exempt from federal drug laws. A higher proportion, 46%, would vote against establishing sites outside of Vancouver's Downtown Eastside, so the referendum on this issue would certainly be a tight one.

Say goodbye to the one-cent coin.

With a 12-point majority, self-governing Canadians would get rid of the one-cent coin. The vote would be 56–44 in favour of abolition.

Don't tax education savings.

Most of us think it's right that money put into a registered savings account to pay for a child's education costs should not be taxed, and should come directly off a person's gross income. Thirty-three percent of Canadians oppose this.

Don't seek clemency for Canadian convicts abroad.

Capital punishment remains a toss-up in this country, with westerners generally in favour and easterners generally opposed. Here, we can find a clear voice only on a related question: If someone gets sentenced to death in a foreign country, they're on their own. Our opinion-poll government would like to be assured that the Canadian citizen got a fair trial, but if they did, it's off to the electric chair with them. By a margin of 53–45, the country wants no more challenging of every death sentence handed to a Canadian.

We would also give the United States permission to detain our citizens in its prison camps if they were suspected of joining insurgent forces overseas—60% of Canadians said it was okay for the United States to keep the Toronto-born Omar Khadr in Guantanamo Bay for six years, and to continue to hold him until their legal processes were complete, rather than returning him to Canada.

Conduct poppies-for-medicine program.

The Canadian people would happily authorize a plan to help Afghan farmers to continue farming poppies and sell their crop to the legitimate pharmaceutical industry rather than into the illegal drug trade. Eighty percent of us think this sounds like a good idea. The same proportion agrees that a pilot project is the best first step. Seventy-five percent of us would be happy to use the fair trade morphine so produced.

Canada opposes the eradication of poppy fields in Afghanistan (by a vote of 54–43). We're particularly against using chemical spraying to do this; 82% oppose the idea of flying over Afghanistan to dump poppy-killing chemicals everywhere, thereby destroying the heroin industry.

Lower the flag more often.

A national referendum held in the midst of a 2008 controversy over the lowering of the Canadian flag on Parliament Hill would have dictated that we lower the Maple Leaf every time a Canadian soldier is killed in the line of duty. Two-thirds wanted to see this happen. Thirty-three percent thought we should lower the flag only on Remembrance Day. (We didn't get people to say how long they thought the flag should stay lowered for.)

Keep guilty ex-citizens out.

When given the chance to express their opinion, Canadians said they didn't want former citizens who've given up their citizenship to return to Canada to serve time in jail after being arrested and con- victed in a foreign country. Okay, if this scenario sounds familiar, it's probably because it was the topic of a major news story a few years back, when the lawyer for a certain disgraced press baron named Conrad Black requested that his client be sent to a minimum-security Canadian prison rather than a facility in the United States. Seven in ten Canadians didn't think this ex-citizen should be allowed back. In the spirit of fairness, presumably, this slammed-door policy must apply to all former Canadians.

Keep a middle-of-the-road refugee policy.

A large portion of Canadians want the country to leap out in front of the pack to extend a helping hand to refugees escaping from danger- ous countries. But this desire is not strong enough to carry a referen- dum vote—the 41% of adults who want Canada to stick its neck out are outnumbered by the 48% who believe we should do whatever the average country does in this regard. With the remaining 11% unwill- ing to comment or arguing that we should do less than the average country, the campaign to do more for refugees would need to come up with a crafty wording for its referendum question to stand much chance of getting a "Yes" vote.

WHAT MUST WE FIX FIRST?

Like any government, a national government-by-poll needs to establish its priorities, especially with so many expensive purchases to consider. Making these choices depends on knowing which bits of our infrastructure are suffering the most, and deciding which bits we care the most about improving. The two decisions are different, of course. For instance, Canadians feel the roads and highways are in a worse condition than hospitals and schools—seventy-five percent of us notice the roads declining in quality or being in desperate need of an overhaul. Fifty-four percent say hospitals are in poor condition. (This majority includes nearly 75% of Albertans, who are generally happier with their roads). Most of us are happy enough with our electricity generation, water, and sewage facilities—if these were made the subject of a national referendum, they'd get a thumbs-up for the status quo. Despite the disapproval concerning our roads, we don't rank fixing these as our highest priority. When it comes to infrastructure, our national priority list is as follows:

1. hospitals
2. schools
3. roads and highways
4. water treatment
5. sewage treatment
6. electricity generation and delivery
7. recreation facilities

Only one in ten Canadians rank improving the local pool or ice rink among their top three priorities. In a national government-by-poll, we'd see infrastructure money going to rec facilities only after we allocate funds to the sewers.

What Changes Our Minds (Warning: This Gets a Bit Technical)

Public opinion is fickle. In case we needed any more proof, we saw just how fickle it can be when we interviewed Canadians about privatizing health care.

A court ruling in Quebec struck down the laws against private health care services. It happened in the middle of 2005, in the waning months of Paul Martin's government. We asked people whether they favoured the court ruling, which effectively made it okay for private insurers to pay for people's cancer tests and hip replacements, rather than making everyone use the public system. This made federal Liberals in Ottawa turn purple in the face. Most people we asked, however, said they approved.

The strongest support for the ruling came from British Columbia and Quebec, where 60% favoured legalizing private health care, versus about 36% who opposed it. Albertans opposed the ruling, but their voices were drowned out by the Quebec and B.C. majorities. Sound strange yet?

If that poll had been a national referendum, the popular will would clearly have been to invite private health care into the Canadian system. It's odd, then, to hear how these same Canadians expressed their thoughts during the remainder of their interview (which was conducted on the Internet). For instance, British Columbians emphatically agreed that the ruling paved the way for a two-tier health care system, would send doctors fleeing from the public system into more lucrative private businesses, and would generally cut people's access to services in public hospitals and clinics. On its own, that's not a total contradiction—perhaps many people see these consequences as what must happen in order to switch to a better system—but it's still weird in Canada to hear people enthusiastically favour a cut in free services and celebrate paying for expensive private ones!

Maybe British Columbians are just highly practical and unromantic about the idea of free health care for all? They might think it's worth giving up on that goal in order to reduce the health care bills paid by governments. But no. The B.C. residents we spoke with also thought the court ruling would drive up the costs for taxpayers, a perception shared by every province except Quebec.

By now, the picture was starting to look really nuts. Here were British Columbians, whom the rest of Canadians sees as the second most left-wing citizens (after Quebecers), saying they want taxpayers to spend more money for fewer services while people pay out of their pockets to get access to the same doctors they once saw for free.

Of course, opinions about politics are complex, and what looks like a contradiction in a poll can actually just be the result of our questions being too simple or clumsy to capture what people are truly thinking—we know this and are always on the lookout for it. However, there's no denying that these answers were starting to sound . . . well . . . surprising.

If you agree with us that those British Columbian opinions seemed not to fit together, maybe you won't be surprised to hear the answer to the next question, which simply asked if the court ruling was a good thing or a bad thing for the country. Suddenly, Quebecers and British Columbians were evenly split—half now said the decision was a bad one for Canada. And in the other provinces, where people had been divided before, Canadians now strongly opposed the court's decision.

On the first question in our interview, the people of Canada had favoured the court ruling by a margin of 6 points—52% vs. 44%.

But by the time we asked our good thing/bad thing question, Canadians opposed the ruling by 11 points—54% vs. 43%!

What had happened is that the questions in between, using hot-button phrases like "two-tier health care" and so on, had changed many people's minds about the court decision. This doesn't mean people were wrong to start off with, just that their sympathies changed when they thought about the issue a different way. Maybe some people supported the ruling at first because they were angry at the governing Liberal Party. And perhaps another set of questions, focusing on the needs and desires of doctors and the problems caused by huge national health care system, would have driven people's opinions the other way into greater support for the court ruling.

In any case, this quick U-turn by the Canadian people in the space of a ten-minute survey shows that our new country governed by opinion polls might have a lot of problems on its hands!

CONCLUSION

Sure, there'd be drawbacks. The first few years could be grim. Some bad decisions would get made, some taxpayer dollars would disappear into a black hole. What else is new?

It would certainly matter who got to write the questions. Maybe we'd need an extra set of opinion polls on what the questions should be before progressing to the next set of opinion polls that actually resulted in laws. It sure sounds like a whole lot of work for pollsters like us . . .

What a great idea!

We hope you've enjoyed finding out many of the big thoughts and tiny details that occupy the lives and minds of so many Canadians. It's a never-ending job for us, one that usually leads to smaller pieces of writing. These facts end up in the headlines of newspaper articles, on the top of a salesperson's PowerPoint presentation, in a press release from a special-interest group, or dropped into a conversation at a bar . . . all over the place, really! Once we've discovered a statistic, there's no telling where it'll end up, so it feels like a kind of reunion to gather so many facts from the last few years together in one place.

Did you manage to get through all the chapters with your individual persona intact? Can you proudly say that you break every mould in the book? Well, we don't mind admitting that there are plenty of surprising Canadians out there, people who make our motto of "Nobody's Unpredictable" such a tough one to live up to. But even if you've proved yourself a maverick this time, don't think we aren't still trying to figure you out. Every day, our pollsters are out there asking more questions, reporting back to us, helping us understand why all kinds of people think what they think and do what they do. Sound alarming? We hope not. After all, the better we all understand each other, in theory, the better we're all going to get along.

PART THREE / HOW WELL DO YOU KNOW WHAT YOU'RE THINKING?

19 / The Great Big Canadian Quiz

We're sure you've been reading this book carefully, page by page, and not skimming over the boring bits, so now that this chapter has come around you're already an expert on the different varieties of Canadians. With all those insights under your belt, it's time to find out just how well you can predict the behaviour of your fellow citizens.

Below, we've devised 100 questions drawn from our surveys on a variety of topics. Your challenge is to answer all of them correctly, without cheating by looking at the answers first. At the end of the quiz, you can use your score to calculate how predictable Canadians are to you.

1. **When Canadians are instructed to take a quiz like this, and told not look at the answers until they've completed the questions, do they usually obey?**
   Yes, 85% of Canadians who take quizzes tell us they honestly tackle these sorts of things without cheating. Five percent admit to cheating just to increase their score. Ten percent usually read the answers without bothering to guess.

2. **Statistically speaking, should you enjoy taking this quiz?**
   Yes, 68% of Canadians enjoy quizzes. It doesn't matter whether you are a man or a woman, rich or poor; you could be an aging great-uncle, a young parent, a middle-aged employee with a university education, an atheist, a Quebecer, or a bachelor. Failing to enjoy this quiz would be decidedly abnormal. Only 10% of Canadians say they are not interested in or they outright hate quizzes.

3. Earlier in the book, we referred to the fact that two-thirds of Canadian adults believe in angels. That amounts to 18 million people. How many of these people say they've had "personal experience" with angels?

(a) 8,000
(b) 80,000
(c) 400,000
(d) 4.5 million

It's the big number, (d). Nearly 5 million Canadians claim to have personally experienced at least one angel. They weren't asked to specify what counts as an angel, however, so it doesn't amount to claiming to have seen a paranormal creature who resembled a human except with wings as well as arms.

4. What is a Canadian more likely to believe in: witchcraft and spells, or God?

Canadians who believe in witchcraft are twice as common as Canadian atheists.

5. How many Canadians bother to obtain a copy of their credit report and review it at least once a year?

(a) Doesn't everybody do this?
(b) Most people do, especially men and seniors.
(c) One in three, regardless of age or gender.
(d) This is a trick question. Ordinary people can't obtain their credit reports, a problem that most Canadians want to see fixed.

It's (c). Regardless of age or gender, only one in three Canadians review their own credit reports annually. And in case you're wondering, a credit report is a file kept by at least one of three credit agencies. It lists your personal information, the bank accounts and credit cards you have, whether you've written any bad cheques, whether you pay your bills on time, and who has inquired about your credit status.

6. **True or false: Every Canadian parent has suffered from influenza at least once.**

   False. Amazingly, 6% of Canadian parents say they've never had the flu.

7. **Do most Canadians keep a "rainy day" savings account, even a small one, to weather a sudden loss of income, debt, or another financial crunch?**

   Only 50% of Canadians keep savings. And 65% of us say our emergency fund is a credit card or a line of credit. Even including the people who do put money aside, more than 80% of Canadians worry that their savings are too small.

8. **How much time does a Canadian adult spend each year, on average, waiting in line?**
   (a) a day
   (b) a week
   (c) a month
   (d) a year

   It's (b), a week. Well, a working week—the average time spent lining up for groceries, movies, and so on, is five days per year. For 7% of the population, however, lining up has become a major pastime. Nearly 2 million Canadians adults claim to spend an hour each day waiting in line, which adds up to 3 working weeks per year.

9. **Smoke alarm manufacturers advise people who live in homes that are more than 10 years old to check the alarm batteries twice a year. Do most people obey?**

   Yes, 62% obediently check their smoke alarm batteries at least twice a year.

10. **How many homeowners mistakenly believe that if smoke alarms are wired into their home's electrical circuits, they never need to be replaced?**
(a) **Nobody is this naïve.**
(b) **one in three**
(c) **the majority**
(d) **This is a trick question—wired-in alarms never need replacing.**

The answer is (b). One in three homeowners figure that if a smoke alarm is powered by the house's electricity rather than by a battery, why replace it? (Smoke alarm manufacturers beg to differ.)

11. **How common is it to remove the batteries from a smoke alarm or pull the whole contraption off the ceiling to silence a false alarm?**
(a) **Very common. Most of us do this.**
(b) **Only the risk-taking half of the population do this.**
(c) **A small, frustrated minority who hate piercing sounds have done this.**
(d) **Hardly anyone does this.**

It's (a) very common. Most Canadians pull their smoke alarms off the ceiling or tear the batteries out from time to time just to shut the alarm up.

12. **And how common is it to forget to replace the alarm after doing this? (Just ballpark a figure of your own.)**

If you guessed that around half of us forget, you're right. Usually people forget for what they call a "short period of time," but 10% of Canadians admit the alarm has remained unplugged or empty of batteries for ages.

13. **True or false: Most Canadians ignore Canada Day.**

    True-ish. Even though people notice Canada Day passing by at the beginning of each July, the majority make no special plans to attend events, celebrate with family or friends, or light any fireworks.

14. **How many e-mails does the average Canadian receive in a week (including unsolicited e-mail)?**

    (a) **50**

    (b) **100**

    (c) **200**

    (d) **500+**

    The average number is 200 e-mails per week.

15. **How many of us continue to open at least 3 spam e-mail messages every week?**

    (a) **a gullible 1% of Internet users**

    (b) **10% of Internet users**

    (c) **25% of Internet users**

    (d) **50% of us**

    Twenty-five percent (c) of Canadian Internet users say they open roughly 3 spam e-mails every week (a tiny fraction, admittedly, of the 130 spams that come in). Most of these people explain they're curious to see what kind of scam or other message is inside the e-mail, while many others say they're genuinely drawn to find out about the product or service.

16. **Who's more likely to make an effort to look into the special offers announced by banks and shop around for the best financial services? Is it men or women?**

    Men. Most men compare financial services and try to figure out if their bank is giving them the best deal. Most women don't bother.

17. **When it comes to money matters—investments, purchases, etc.—are men or women more inclined to make decisions on the spur of the moment?**
Women are much more likely to. In fact, most women say they like making spur-of-the-moment decisions. Most men don't like it.

18. **How many parents describe their kids (aged 6 to 12) as "picky eaters"?**
(a) **All kids aged 6 to 12 are picky eaters.**
(b) **Half of the parents say they've got a picky kid.**
(c) **A quarter of these kids are picky eaters.**
(d) **How do you eat a "picky" anyway?**
The answer is (c), one-quarter. Roughly the same number of parents argue, or at least disagree, with their kids over what they're going to eat. It's also common to complain that kids are too slow in the morning to have time to eat a balanced breakfast every day, and that three food groups is too much food. One third of young kids don't like to eat at all first thing in the morning.

19. **True or false: Most Canadian adults have not prepared a will.**
False, but only just. Forty-five percent of adults don't have a will, a figure bloated by the fact that hardly anyone under the age of 34 bothers to prepare one. Even in the 35 to 54 age group, however, 40% haven't written a statement of their final wishes.

20. **Is a woman more or less likely than a man to have a detailed discussion with her family about her "final wishes"?**
Most women have done this; most men haven't.

21. **Who is more likely to cook a Thanksgiving turkey? A husband with only a high school diploma or a husband with a university degree?**

Regardless of education and income, the woman of the household almost always cooks the turkey for Thanksgiving. The only noticeable difference in responses is due to the fact that university-educated people are apparently a bit less likely to eat turkey. Three in ten men have never cooked a turkey.

22. **How common is it for a woman to carve a turkey that a man has cooked?**
(a) **This has never happened in Canada.**
(b) **This is normal in one household out of a hundred.**
(c) **This occurs regularly in one in ten households.**
(d) **Almost half of the women we spoke with say they do this all the time.**

   The answer is (b). If you're a woman who carves a turkey cooked by a man who lives in your house, you're extremely rare.

23. **Where are boys and girls most likely to get equal access to good sports and recreation facilities?**
(a) **Alberta**
(b) **New Brunswick**
(c) **Prince Edward Island**
(d) **Nova Scotia**

   It's (c), Prince Edward Island. In P.E.I., 66% of residents strongly agree that boys and girls should have equal access in their community. By contrast, only 34% of Nova Scotians strongly agree, as do 36% of New Brunswickers. Alberta scores a bit better, with 45% completely confident that boys shouldn't get more access than girls. But none of the other provinces comes close to P.E.I. on this score.

24. **What percentage of Canadians participated in Earth Hour 2009?**
   a) 39%
   b) 60%
   c) 72%
   d) 81%

   The answer is (b) 60%—and don't forget to turn the lights off on your way out.

25. **Where are you least likely to see kids playing unsupervised in the neighbourhood?**
   (a) **Vancouver**
   (b) **Toronto**
   (c) **Winnipeg**
   (d) **Montreal**

   In (a), Vancouver. While 83% of Montrealers feel it's safe to let kids play in the neighbourhood with minimal supervision, only 63% of Vancouver adults feel comfortable with this. In Toronto, 70% of adults think their neighbourhood is pretty safe for kids. In Winnipeg, 75% say it's safe. Interestingly, even in the Vancouver area, only 10% of adults "strongly" feel it's unsafe to leave kids playing outside with minimal supervision. Inner-city parents show more caution than their suburban counterparts. In downtown Toronto, for instance, the comfort levels on this issue drop to 63%; in the suburban metro area, 79% of adults say the neighbourhood is safe for kids.

26. **Which major city's police force gets top marks from locals?**
   Victoria, where one-third of the population strongly agree the police do a great job. Calgary and Toronto police also get abundant praise from local residents.

27. **Where would a provincial premier win the most voter support with a speech attacking judges for handing out lenient sentences to criminals?**

(a) Calgary

(b) Ottawa

(c) Halifax

(d) Victoria

This would be a particularly good speech to give in (c), Halifax, where nine in ten people think judges are too lenient. Calgary is remarkably pro-judge by comparison: One in four residents approve of judicial sentencing. Other good cities in which to criticize judges include Montreal, Vancouver, and Edmonton, where roughly eight in ten think sentencing is too lenient.

28. **You're invited to dinner with a family from Quebec. Which of the following statements is more likely to be a faux pas?**

(a) **"I think all the opposition to having police surveillance cameras in public places is so dumb and flimsy."**

(b) **"It's racist to claim that certain ethnic groups are more responsible for crime."**

Both statements would be unadvisable. Quebecers oppose surveillance cameras in public places much more than other Canadians (except those living on P.E.I. or in Newfoundland and Labrador). Quebecers also overwhelmingly reject the idea that people from certain ethnic groups are particularly likely to commit crimes—73% disagree with this, compared to 51% of Ontarians, and 39% of Manitobans. It's a bad idea to voice opinion (b) at a dinner table in Manitoba unless you're willing to offend your hosts by implying that they're racist.

29. **Where will you find the most people who think marijuana should not be a criminal offence?**

(a) **British Columbia**

(b) **Atlantic Canada**

(c) **Ontario**

(d) **Quebec**

The answer is (c) Quebec (63%), just behind British Columbia (59%), Atlantic Canada (56%) and the rest of the country (tied at 50%).

30. **In Saskatchewan and Manitoba, Céline Dion is in tenth place among the figures who best define the country, behind a woman who isn't even Canadian. Who do you think that person is?**

Queen Elizabeth II. We were unable to reach Her Majesty for a comment on how she felt about being ahead of Céline on the Prairie list.

31. **True or false: Most Canadians don't worry about terrorist attacks against this country.**

True. Even in the heart of Toronto, the people who are nervous about terrorism are significantly outnumbered by those who are confident that Canada will suffer no major attacks anytime soon. The city with the lowest fear of terrorism is Victoria, where only a quarter of residents feel unsure about Canada's safety.

32. **Who are the most tolerant Canadians, New Brunswickers or British Columbians?**

When it comes to conflicting moral values, New Brunswickers are Canada's most tolerant citizens; 70% think people should be allowed to live according to their own moral standards and not be expected to conform. British Columbians are less likely to feel this way, sharing a similar level of ambivalence (57%–59%) with Alberta, Ontario, P.E.I., Quebec, and Saskatchewan.

33. **Which province gives itself the highest approval ratings for theatre and ballet facilities?**
(a) **British Columbia**
(b) **Alberta**
(c) **Manitoba**
(d) **Ontario**

That would be (b), Alberta, where 58% say the province gives a good home to high-cultural activities. That's just a whisker ahead of B.C., which gets a 56% approval rating, followed by Manitoba (52%) and Ontario (50%). Nova Scotia has the lowest score, at 42%.

34. **In which province is Jim Carrey rated among the ten most definitive Canadians of all time?**

Alberta. He's just two spots behind Stephen Harper on the province's top ten list.

35. **Who would Canadians choose to pass the Olympic torch to if they could?**

Terry Fox (44%) was tops, followed by Wayne Gretzky (14%), former prime minister Pierre Trudeau (12%), Celine Dion (7%), Gordie Howe (5%), and Oscar Peterson (3%).

36. **Where is it most socially acceptable for a couple to have sex out of wedlock?**
(a) **Vancouver**
(b) **Winnipeg**
(c) **Montreal**
(d) **Halifax**

That's (c), Montreal, where 86% have no problem with sex outside of marriage. Seventy-five percent of Winnipeggers say this is okay. Twenty percent of Winnipeggers (and the same proportion of Edmontonians) believe you should marry someone before having sex with them.

37. **Who is the least likely to approve of sex before marriage?**
(a) a young adult in Toronto
(b) a young adult in Ottawa
(c) an adult earning more than $60,000 a year
(d) a rural Canadian

> It's (a); the young adult in Toronto, where 69% think unmarried
> people can have sex, compared to 83% of young Ottawans, 75% of
> rich adults, and 71% of rural Canadians.

38. **If you're an urban resident who feels overwhelmed by the
so-called "information age," you might plan to leave the city and
move to a rural area—good idea or bad idea?**

> Bad idea. Rural Canadians apparently suffer from an excess of
> frustrating or confusing information just as much as urbanites do.

39. **Who suffers most from "information overload"—that is, the
feeling that life overwhelms you with things you're supposed to
know, understand, or respond to?**
(a) Newfoundlanders
(b) low-income Canadians
(c) young Ottawa adults
(d) readers of this book

> Okay, we can't exactly survey the readers of this book and publish
> the results inside it—in fact, just the thought of how that could
> work is giving us a headache. But we figure that even an important
> book like this one wouldn't have such an overwhelming effect
> on somebody's life, so that leaves (c) young Ottawa adults as
> the most information-overloaded people here. Among Ottawa
> residents between the ages of 18 and 34, 40% often feel overloaded,
> compared to 34% of low-income Canadians, and just 21%
> of Newfoundlanders. In fact, Newfoundland and Labrador is

apparently the best province to inhabit if you want less information to deal with. (Caveat: people in Nunavut and the territories did not participate in this survey.) Only 37% of young Ottawa adults claim to have escaped the clutches of information overload so far.

40. **Who is more stressed out: Prince Edward Islanders or downtown Torontonians?**

Sixty percent of Prince Edward Islanders are stressed out nowadays, compared to 56% of downtown Torontonians.

41. **True or false: Day-to-day living in Vancouver is quite stressful for most residents.**

False. Only 20% of Vancouverites find their lives stressful. Sixty percent disagree that Vancouver living can be quite a stress. Stress levels may be fractionally higher in the province's capital, Victoria, although the difference is within the margin of error for our polls.

42. **Which is the most stressful city to live in, according to young adults?**

(a) **Toronto**

(b) **Ottawa**

(c) **Montreal**

(d) **Calgary**

That's (c), Montreal, where 34% of young adults find the city a stressful place. This compares to about 22% of young adults in Ottawa and Toronto. (This doesn't mean Montrealers are more stressed out in general, just that more of them consider the city itself to be a cause of stress. Apparently, stressed-out young people in Toronto and Ottawa blame other things for their stress, such as their job or the state of the world today.) Young adults in Calgary are the least likely to find their city stressful—just 16% of them make this complaint.

43. **True or false: Most young adults in Vancouver eat their dinner in front of the television.**

True. So do most young adults in Ottawa. This habit is less common among their peers in Calgary and Edmonton, however.

44. **True or false: Ontarians eat more TV dinners than Newfoundlanders.**

True again. Fifty percent of Ontario residents eat their dinner most often in front of the television. Only 34% of Newfoundlanders do this regularly.

45. **In which city are you most likely to find a family sitting down together for dinner at home?**
  (a) **Calgary**
  (b) **Toronto**
  (c) **Montreal**
  (d) **Halifax**

It's (c), Montreal, where 75% of families do this almost every evening. Only 65% of Toronto families share the same routine, while 60% of Calgary families regularly eat their dinner together around a table.

46. **You have two friends, one from Ontario and one from British Columbia. You have one carrot. Which friend should you give the carrot to?**

Well, of course there might be a few factors you'd want to consider, such as which friend looks more hungry, which one has already eaten some vegetables today (probably your B.C. friend), and which person asked for the carrot more politely, but all else being equal, your friend from Ontario is more likely to love carrots. Ontarians mention the carrot as their favourite vegetable twice as often as British Columbians do.

47. Who's more likely to object to Camilla Parker-Bowles one day taking the title of "Queen of Canada"?

(a) a man

(b) a woman

A woman. Seventy-one percent of Canadian women don't want Camilla to take the title of Queen; only 58% of men object to her doing this.

48. How common is it to consume vegetables less than four times a week?

(a) only common among scurvy sufferers

(b) very rare—as rare as saying elected politicians do a great job of debating important issues

(c) quite common—as common as owning a hand-held electronic game

(d) You mean some people eat vegetables four times a week?

It's (c), quite common. Nearly a quarter of us eat vegetables three times a week or less. Put another way, that means someone who belongs to this group eats zero vegetables four days out of each week.

49. How many new Canadians view the overall quality of life in this country as better than that of their country of origin?

(a) 65%

(b) 86%

(c) all of them

Answer: (b) 86%, with 44% saying it is "much better" in Canada. Nine percent say it's about the same, and 5% believe it's better in their country of origin.

50. **True or false: Most Canadians would rather not see their government apologize for all the transgressions and mistakes committed in the past.**

False. Two-thirds of Canadians think it is appropriate to issue formal apologies for historical wrongs such as the mistreatment of Japanese-Canadians in the 1940s, the "head tax" levied on Chinese-Canadians, and the residential school system that aimed to erase Aboriginal cultures.

51. **Which region is home to the biggest proportion of Canadians who don't celebrate Christmas?**
   (a) **British Columbia**
   (b) **Ontario**
   (c) **Quebec**
   (d) **Atlantic Canada**

   It's (a), British Columbia, where 10% of the population don't celebrate the holiday.

52. **What's a Quebecer more likely to call Christmas: a time to reflect on the birth of Jesus, a nice festive season in the middle of winter, or a time for family get-togethers?**

   Most Quebecers (72%) say Christmas is for family get-togethers.

53. **Which province objected more strongly when the Canadian government proposed withholding tax credits from independent films deemed offensive or "contrary to public policy"?**
   (a) **Alberta**
   (b) **Quebec**

   Alberta (a). Fifty-seven percent of Albertans oppose such government interference in the arts.

54. **Who complains the most about the quality of their roads?**
(a) **Prairie Canadians**
(b) **Quebecers**
(c) **British Columbians**
(d) **Ontarians**

It's (a) the people on the Prairies. Among Saskatchewaners and Manitobans, 93% say the roads are "declining" (in terms of quality, not downward slopes) or in desperate condition. Quebecers are relatively upbeat by comparison, with 86% complaining about the quality of the roads. Almost 50% of British Columbians describe their roads as being in good or excellent condition. Forty-two percent of Albertans say their roads and highways are good.

55. **Where are people least inclined to praise the quality of Canada's health care system?**
(a) **Alberta**
(b) **the Prairies**
(c) **Ontario**
(d) **the Atlantic provinces**

That would be (d), the Atlantic provinces, where only 28% rate it as excellent or very good, followed closely by the Prairies at 29%, Alberta at 34%, and Ontario at 37%.

56. **Are Canadians growing more confident or less confident in the courts of justice?**

More confident, it would seem. In 1997, barely 50% of Canadians expressed confidence in the courts. Ten years later, 62% said they felt confident. In fact, the number of people who said they felt "very confident" doubled to 13%.

57. **Do most Canadians feel good about the way the parole system works in this country?**

    No. But even this seems to be improving. In 1997, only 25% of Canadians expressed confidence in the parole system. By 2007, this had leapt up to 41%.

58. **What percentage of Canadians sent money online between June 2008 and June 2009, either through a bank's website or a third party?**
    (a) 17%
    (b) 28%
    (c) 33%
    (d) 48%

    It's (b)—28%. The reasons given for these payments include: covering the share of a restaurant bill (56%), splitting the cost of a gift for a wedding or a shower (44%), sending cash as a gift (40%), pitching in for a portion of a weekend getaway (22%), purchasing concert tickets (19%), paying for team dues or recreational activities (16%), or simply sending money to somebody abroad (8%).

59. **Are Canadians getting more wary about inviting immigrants to live here?**

    No. Compared to a decade ago, we are more welcoming to immigrants. In 1998, 60% of us said that Canada should take in the same number of immigrants as other similar-sized developed countries do, while 15% thought we should be taking in more. By 2007, those numbers had changed to 49% and 23%, respectively.

60. **What's more important to the Canadian public overall?**
    (a) encouraging more acceptance of minority customs and languages
    (b) encouraging minority cultures to change in order to fit in with mainstream Canada

The answer is (b), and the numbers for this have stayed steady over the last 20 years. Six out of ten Canadians figure the bigger priority for this country should be encouraging minority groups to learn how to be like the majority of Canadians.

61. **Were Canadians more sympathetic to refugees 20 years ago than they are now?**
No. In 1987, 22% of Canadians wanted the country to do less for foreign refugees than other countries do. By 2007, only 8% expressed this opinion, while the number of people who thought we should do more than most countries nearly doubled, to 41%.

62. **What's happening to Canadians' views about euthanasia (i.e., assisted suicide) for terminally ill patients?**
(a) **We are becoming more supportive of it.**
(b) **We are growing more opposed to it.**
(c) **We are keeping a steady attitude.**
The answer is (c). People support or oppose doctor-assisted suicide in the same proportions today as they have for decades: 70% say it's a good idea; 25% are opposed to it; the remaining few aren't sure.

63. **Do Canadians recognize a "right to die"?**
Yes. Seventy-five percent of Canadians agree that people have a right to die rather than endure the full course of a terminal disease.

64. **Are people growing more or less concerned about foreign ownership of Canadian companies?**
Slightly more. In 1989, 50% of Canadians we spoke to saw this as a real problem. By 2007, this had crept up to 56%.

65. **How many Canadians think universities ought to work more closely with the world of business?**
(a) almost everybody
(b) half the population
(c) very few

Almost everybody (a) agrees that universities and colleges, and even schools for younger people, should get closer to the business community to produce the "highly skilled people needed to sustain and improve Canada's economy." Only 5% of Canadians disagree with this.

66. **Who is most likely to think that a laid-off worker needs theoretical education more than practical skills training?**
(a) a young adult
(b) a middle-aged person
(c) someone born before 1950

Young adults (a) are the most likely to believe this. Fifteen percent of them say this idea makes a lot of sense, compared to 4% of those over 55.

67. **Do most Canadians think the country is outpacing other nations when it comes to competing for wealth and inventing new products?**

No way: 71% of men and 62% of women think Canada is falling behind.

68. **What percentage of Canadians regularly smoke cigarettes?**
(a) 5%
(b) 2.5%

(c) 60%

(d) 20%

It's (d): Twenty percent of Canadians regularly smoke cigarettes. Seventy-five percent of those people want to quit or reduce their smoking.

69. Who's more likely to dine on unhealthy food—a man or a woman?

A man. A third of the men we spoke with admitted to regularly eating unhealthy stuff, compared to just a quarter of the women.

70. How many Canadian men regularly drink alcohol?

(a) three-quarters

(b) just over half

(c) just under half

(d) one quarter

It's (c), just under half. Only a quarter of Canadian women regularly drink booze.

71. Who's the least likely to spend more than 90 minutes per day cleaning their home?

(a) a young adult

(b) a university graduate

(c) somebody with no kids in the house

(d) a man

It's (b), a university graduate. Only 2% of people with university degrees spend more than an 90 minutes on housecleaning on a typical day, compared to 5% of men, 6% of young adults, and 8% of people with no kids.

72. **How much do most Canadians spend each week on coffee in the morning?**
(a) nothing
(b) up to $10
(c) between $10 and $20
(d) over $20

It's (a). Most Canadians don't buy a cup of coffee in the morning. Now, if we asked just men, or young adults, or university graduates, we'd find that half of them spend up to $10 throughout the week. But they are balanced out by women, older Canadians, and less educated people, most of whom don't buy cups of coffee.

73. **True or false: Canadians are more likely than Americans to believe they will receive timely and effective medical treatment if they get sick.**

False. Only 56% of Canadians are confident of good treatment, versus 71% of Americans.

74. **Okay. Two rooms in the house need cleaning, the kitchen and the bedroom. You have two volunteers, one aged 25 and one aged 60. Which of the two rooms do they probably want to clean?**
(a) Both want to clean the bedroom.
(b) The young one wants to do the dishes in the kitchen, while the older one would rather head for the bedroom and pick up the dirty underwear and make the bed.
(c) It's like (b) said, only the other way round.
(d) Both want to get the bedroom job.

Your best bet is (c). The most popular room in the house for young adults, when it comes to cleaning, is the bedroom. Among older adults, it's the kitchen.

75. **Do most people enjoy housecleaning?**

    Strangely enough, yes, they do! Fifty-four percent of Canadians claim to enjoy housecleaning at least a bit. Sixty-six percent of people who didn't finish high school say they actually enjoy housecleaning, which may explain why they spend so much of the day doing it.

76. **Who is more likely to favour extracting oil from Alberta's tar sands—men or women?**

    Men, 41% of whom think the oil companies should charge full steam ahead without waiting until cleaner methods of extraction are invented. Only 30% of women agree with this opinion.

77. **How many Canadians think we should have the same environmental and climate change policies as the United States?**
    (a) **one in ten**
    (b) **five in ten**
    (c) **nine in ten**

    That's (c): Nine in ten Canadians want the same climate change policies in both countries, although they don't necessarily want to switch over to the latest American policy—instead, they want the two countries to work together to harmonize their plans.

78. **How optimistic are Canadians that the economy will be environmentally sustainable within their lifetime?**

    Pretty optimistic. In fact, 60% expect this will happen. Understandably, the least confident group is people over 55, but even these people usually say they'll see an environmentally sustainable economy before they die.

79. **Do Canadians figure they're already doing their fair share to fight climate change, on a personal level?**
Yes, 85% claim to be doing their fair share already.

80. **How many Canadians are doing more than most other Canadians to save the environment?**
(a) **Obviously just a few of them, otherwise this question doesn't make any sense.**
(b) **Most Canadians are doing more than most other Canadians.**
The answer is (b). Well, obviously it can't really be (b) because that just doesn't add up. But according to public opinion polls, 70% believe they're doing "more than most" to help the environment.

81. **What would Albertans rather see their government spend money on: research into renewable and clean energy, or oil and gas exploration and development?**
Renewables, by far: 78% want to see government investment in this area, while just 11% think oil and gas development is a better place for taxpayer dollars. Only 2% don't think the government should give money to either area.

82. **Canada is made up of ten provinces and some territories. Who's more likely to know how many territories there are—a younger person or an older person?**
Most young adults know that Canada has three territories. Most older ones still think Canada has one or two.

83. **Who's more likely to know that more Inuit live in Canada today than at any time since this country's birth—a younger person or an older person?**

An older person. Only 40% of younger adults know this; 60% of older Canadians do.

84. **How many Canadians would prefer to see the government focus attention on the northern territories of Canada rather than on the activities of the United States?**
(a) **Hardly anybody thinks this is sensible.**
(b) **We're split down the middle—50% think our focus should be northward, 50% say southward.**
(c) **Most Canadians want our government to turn its back on the United States and face north.**
(d) **Canadians unite—we all want to have a government that cares more about the northern territories than about the United States.**
The answer is (c): 75% of Canadians think the government needs to pay more attention to Canada's North and less to the United States. Among those with a high school education or less, 30% strongly agree with this idea, while university graduates are more reluctant: only 16% strongly agree, and 33% disagree.

85. **Who is most likely to expect life and habitat in the North will soon be destroyed by climate change?**
(a) **a new Canadian**
(b) **a man**
(c) **a low-income Canadian**
(d) **a young adult**
The pessimism of the young strikes again—the answer is (d): 80% of young people expect that climate change will soon destroy life in the North. Across the country, Atlantic Canadians are the most pessimistic about this, with 85% of the people in that region convinced the end is nigh.

86. **How many Canadians have visited one of the northern territories?**
(a) one in ten
(b) two in ten
(c) five in ten
(d) Most people have visited the North at least once.

    It's (a). Roughly one in ten Canadians have visited either Yukon, the Northwest Territories, or Nunavut.

87. **We asked Canadians whom they would want to pass the Olympic Torch to, if they had the honour of carrying it for a while. Who was the most popular choice?**
(a) Margaret Atwood
(b) Pierre Trudeau
(c) Wayne Gretzky
(d) Terry Fox

    The answer is (d), Terry Fox, by a mile: 44% chose Terry, 14% chose Wayne, 12% chose Pierre, and 2% chose Margaret (causing a three-way tie among Margaret, Hayley Wickenheiser, and Maurice Richard. Perhaps they would have to carry the torch together when it came to their turn).

88. **Who are the biggest fans of Canada's Food Guide?**
(a) middle-aged people
(b) older people
(c) men
(d) women

    It's (b), the older people, 88% of whom agree that the Food Guide helps them meet their energy and nutrient needs in order to fuel an active lifestyle. Seventy-eight percent of young people appreciate the Food Guide and 22% of men say it doesn't help them.

89. Who's more likely to believe that weight-loss or muscle-building supplements are necessary to get the most out of a physical workout?

(a) a man
(b) a university graduate
(c) a low-income person
(d) an Atlantic Canadian

It's (c), the low-income person. Roughly 25% of this group think these supplements lead to more weight loss or muscle-building than regular old natural foodstuffs. University graduates are the least convinced—only 12% believe the supplements work better than normal food.

90. Two guys are at the gym. One is constantly drinking water while he works out. The other, not so much. The water-drinker is . . .

(a) probably from Quebec
(b) probably from British Columbia

The answer is (a), from Quebec, where 86% of people put a lot of faith in drinking as much water as possible while working out. Twenty-five percent of British Columbians don't see the point.

91. Who gets more blame from Canadians for the Middle East conflict between Israel and Palestine?

(a) Israel
(b) Palestine

It's (b), Palestine: 43% of Canadians who watch the news about the Middle East conflict blame Palestinians, while only 18% blame Israelis. Another 40% of the people who follow these events say they don't know who is to blame, or they blame neither side in particular.

92. **How common is it for men to feel their body weight is "about right"?**
(a) Most men feel this way.
(b) Most men think they're overweight.
(c) Hardly any men worry about their own weight—they're too busy worrying about their girlfriend's/wife's weight!

It's (b). Most men consider themselves overweight. But 44% figure their weight is just about right. Twenty-five percent of men say they don't worry about this topic.

93. **Who's more likely to believe in angels?**
(a) someone with kids
(b) someone without kids

The person with kids is more likely to believe this—three-quarters of parents believe in angels, compared to just two-thirds of people who don't have kids in the house.

94. **Among people who believe in angels, who's the most likely to think of angels as heavenly creatures with wings?**
(a) a Prairie Canadian
(b) a woman
(c) someone who didn't finish high school
(d) an older Canadian

It's the Prairie Canadian. Seventy-five percent of the people in Saskatchewan and Manitoba believe that angels exist, and 25% of these people think of them as paranormal creatures with wings. Only 15% of the women who believe in angels think they have wings. Only 14% of the high-school dropouts, and 11% of the older people who believe in angels, agree.

95. **How many dads know how to change a diaper when their first child is born?**
(a) 80%
(b) 40%
(c) 20%

   It's (a). Eighty percent of dads claim that they knew how to change a diaper when their first child was born. Even more—88%—say they knew how to burp the baby.

96. **Which province has the most confident first-time dads?**
(a) British Columbia
(b) Saskatchewan
(c) Quebec

   It's (c): 87% of Quebec dads claim that they felt "completely prepared" for parenthood when the first baby showed up, compared to 61% of the first-time dads in B.C. and 53% of the ones in Saskatchewan.

97. **Where are men the least inclined to agree that their wife had a wealth of information before and after the birth of their first child?**
(a) British Columbia
(b) Alberta
(c) Quebec
(d) Atlantic Canada

   It's (b), Alberta, where only 28% of men strongly agree that their wife was a great source of information. Meanwhile, 86% of Quebecers, 83% of British Columbians, and 84% of Atlantic Canadian dads considered their wives a great source of knowledge.

98. How many Canadian drivers disapprove of using a cellphone while driving?

(a) nine out of ten

(b) Most disapprove.

(c) two out of ten

(d) Almost nobody disapproves.

The answer is (a). Nine out of ten Canadian drivers disapprove of using a cellphone while driving (a vehicle, that is. Canadians are mightily impressed by someone who can use their cellphone while driving a golf ball).

99. How many Canadian drivers admit to using their cellphone while driving?

(a) nine out of ten

(b) Most admit this.

(c) two out of ten

(d) Almost nobody admits this.

Most Canadian drivers (b) admit they've used their cellphone while operating a vehicle.

100. What are drivers most likely to do?

(a) eat a meal while driving

(b) drive while sleepy

(c) drive while putting on makeup

It's (a). Thirty percent of drivers admit that they've done this. Albertans are the most likely to eat while driving—42% say they have. Only 24% of Quebecers admit to eating while driving, though they didn't say if their reluctance to do this was due to the risk of driving badly, or to the risk of not fully appreciating the food.

Scores

Fewer than 33 correct answers

Take heart. It's a great thing to live in a world that is constantly mysterious.

33–66 correct answers

You have very good instincts for recognizing typical behaviours in your fellow Canadians. Unfortunately, you also have a strong instinct for making the wrong guess. The best advice we can give you is to hire a pollster to guide you through any moments when you feel uncertain about the thoughts of the people around you.

67–100 correct answers

Congratulations! You can confidently live in Canada without meeting many unpleasant surprises—in fact, if you're in the upper part of this category, you won't often be surprised at all. May we suggest it's time to consider a career in marketing or politics. Or if those don't appeal to you, perhaps you should come work for us!

A book on polling wouldn't be complete without a pie chart, but that would be very unCanadian, since we consume more donuts than pies. In fact, Canadians consume more donuts per capita than any other people on the planet. So we felt it was only right to put a donut chart on the cover. And for our final poll before sending the book off to the printer, we asked Canadians what their favourite kind of donut is. Here's what they told us:

What's your favourite donut?

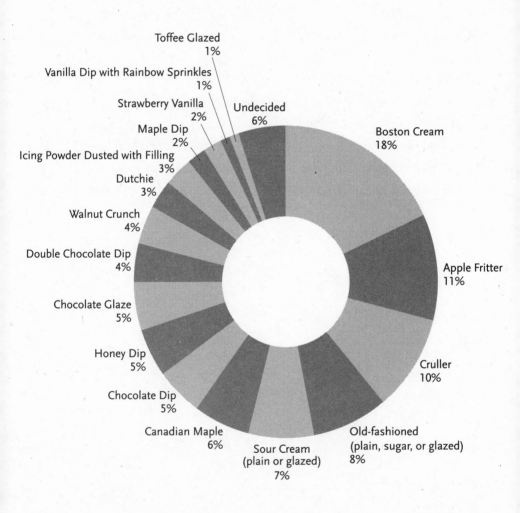

Toffee Glazed
1%

Vanilla Dip with Rainbow Sprinkles
1%

Strawberry Vanilla
2%

Undecided
6%

Maple Dip
2%

Icing Powder Dusted with Filling
3%

Dutchie
3%

Walnut Crunch
4%

Double Chocolate Dip
4%

Chocolate Glaze
5%

Honey Dip
5%

Chocolate Dip
5%

Canadian Maple
6%

Sour Cream
(plain or glazed)
7%

Boston Cream
18%

Apple Fritter
11%

Cruller
10%

Old-fashioned
(plain, sugar, or glazed)
8%